What People Are S
The AGILE MI

I cannot stress how important it is to help teams and organisations become more Agile minded rather than just follow a process.

~Geoff Watts, Leadership Coach, author of *Scrum Mastery*

Examines the most misunderstood part of creating a new mode of working in a world of increased complexity and opportunity.

~Ryan Martens, CTO and Founder, Rally

Once you get the Agile mind-set and have enough reference examples, applying it to your own context follows naturally. Gil Broza has organized its components in an approachable, easy-to-follow structure, accompanying each component by plenty of vivid stories.

~Guy Nachimson, Agile Practitioner

There has been a lot of talk about the Agile mind-set; finally we've a book that distills down the core principles required to embrace it, keeping the whole system in mind.

~Naresh Jain, Founder, Agile India

You won't beat the status quo if you don't think differently. The Agile Mind-Set *gets to the heart of what it is that makes Agile more than just another process.*

~Dan Snyder, Director and Consultant, iTCS Consulting Services

This truly inspirational book captures how an Agilist looks at work and life. This is not a "how to" book, it is a book on why Agilists are successful.

~Mark Kilby, Agile Coach, Sonatype

By sharing the values, beliefs, and principles that make Agile effective, I immediately helped team members I've worked with for years connect with each other, their work, and the company in new and more effective ways.

~Craig Dial, Lead ScrumMaster, cPanel

This straightforward, easy, and engaging read gives practical advice to hone your Agile skills. As an established Agile practitioner it has helped me to reevaluate and challenge my mind-set.

~Dinah Davis, Senior Development Manager

The Agile Mind-Set shows us how to create a team dynamic that can deliver extraordinary results while keeping the customer engaged along the way. This dynamic doesn't happen on its own. Fortunately we have here a treasure trove of insights, principles, and practical advice to help us lead our teams to great results.

~Andy Norman, Senior VP Delivery, Mobiquity

Gil Broza clarifies a phrase that's never been well-defined: Agile mind-set. His thoughtful, comprehensive approach to defining the many dimensions of mind-set as well as why it supports teams' and organizations' meeting their goals is an important contribution to making Agile adoptions and transformations possible.

~Diana Larsen, FutureWorks Consulting, coauthor of *Liftoff* and *Agile Retrospectives*

Do you struggle to "be Agile" rather than just "do Agile"? This book provides deep insights and practical techniques to apply an Agile mind-set to help people move work from concept to completion.

~Declan Whelan, Agile Coach, Leanintuit

I like how this book doesn't tell you what to do. It helps you to see how to think differently. This is a much-needed catalyst to help teams learn how to be Agile and not just go through the motions of certain Agile practices.

~Paul Carvalho, President and Consultant, Quality Driven Inc.

This is the book that I didn't know I was looking for.

~Gitte Klitgaard, Agile Coach, Native Wired

Gil Broza respectfully rewords and expands the original definition of Agile into a comprehensive and cohesive set of values, principles, and beliefs. Upon this foundation, he offers the reader manifestations of Agile thinking in various aspects of people and work, backed by experience and cases. This is a very balanced and cohesive work, with a clear structure and good flow. It is bound to improve your understanding of Agile, and what it is that might make Agile work in your context.

~Gunther Verheyen, Shepherding Professional Scrum at Scrum.org and author of *Scrum: A Pocket Guide*

As an Agile leader and change agent, this book helped me to fill up my transformation toolbox, realign my personal thoughts, and reinvigorate me to practice Agile like I mean it.

~Vanessa Roberts, Project Manager, ScrumMaster and Agile Leader

By getting us to focus on values, beliefs, and principles rather than specific frameworks and practices, Gil Broza exposes the real reasons that Agile works, as well as the reasons when it does not work.

~Jeff McKenna, Agile Mentor, Coach of the first Scrum team (in 1993!)

Great for newcomers but also excellent at stoking the Agile fire of established practitioners.

~Mike Syms, Product Owner

Straightforward and no-nonsense, the book is filled with pragmatic patterns and practices to help navigate and conquer the complex world of software development.

~Stacey Louie, President, Silicon Valley Agile Leadership Network and CEO, Bratton & Co.

The
AGILE MIND-SET

Making Agile Processes Work

GIL BROZA

Forewords by **Jim Highsmith** *and* **Linda Rising**

The publisher offers discounts on this book when ordered in quantity for bulk purchases or special sales, which may include electronic versions and/or custom covers and content particular to your business, training goals, marketing focus, and branding interests. For more information, please contact:

Gil Broza
(416) 302-8120
support@3PVantage.com

Published by 3P Vantage Media

ISBN: 978-1514769331

Book design: Heather Kirk, GFSstudio.com

Editing: Mark Woodworth, editmarks.weebly.com

Printed in the United States of America.

CONTENTS

FOREWORD

by Jim Highsmith

To succeed at Agile development, individuals and organizations must both *do* Agile and *be* Agile. The latter has proven to be difficult. We have so many cool and alluring Agile practices — daily standup meetings, test-driven development, story cards, backlog building, pairing — and the list continues to expand as we reach the 15th year since the signing of the Agile Manifesto. Unfortunately, Being Agile doesn't come with a nice set of instructions that can be memorized and applied. Being Agile is a mind-set — the thought process behind our behaviors.

A mind-set — some may say culture — is human and therefore messy. Maybe that's why we try to ignore it and get on with the more "rational" side of Agile. As Gil Broza aptly points out, an Agile mind-set combines values, beliefs, and principles that in turn guide how processes and practices are implemented. Values are what we think are important, whether it's low cost or happy teams. But values sneak up on us because many of them are unspoken. Effective Agile leaders help their teams translate their values from implicit to explicit to uncover both aligned and unaligned values.

Gil defines beliefs as "something you hold to be true but haven't proven, and perhaps can't prove rigorously." If I believe that people are basically lazy and need to be "motivated" by managers (Douglas McGregor's Theory X), then that belief permeates my approach to all personnel issues — from hiring to performance reviews. On the other hand, if I believe people are motivated by purpose, mastery, and autonomy (Daniel Pink), then my approach to people management will be entirely different.

Principles define how work gets done and drive choice of practices and processes. As Gil points out, one set of values and beliefs might generate several versions of principles. The Agile principles are derived from a stated set of values and beliefs. I love Gil's short names for Agile principles such as: Cadence, Reliability, Simplicity, Shippable, Quality, Time-Box, and Collaboration.

Talking about the various aspects of mind-set has the potential to be interesting, but is often boring. Gil skirts this tendency by explaining the practical aspects of mind-set and how it applies to critical activities such as planning work and building teams. Furthermore, Gil's stories and examples from his extensive experience with Agile teams keep you reading.

Organizations often fail at Agile because they don't progress past rule-based Agile 101. They flounder in what I've called "prescriptive agility" (an oxymoron, of course) where rules rule: do this, don't do that. While a prescriptive approach may be fine for early learning, "adaptive agility" — the adjective shouldn't be necessary — remains the goal. The ability to learn and adapt defines true agility, and it comes from understanding values, beliefs, and principles. By focusing on these, Gil does a great job of showing you how to achieve adaptive agility.

As an example, Gil and I once worked with a company that had implemented Agile in its software teams and wanted to build Agile hardware teams. Some of the practices translated directly (collaborative teams) while others didn't (test-driven development). However, when we thought about the principle behind the practice, we were successful in the adaptation. In this particular case, the company completely changed its approach to hardware testing based on the principles and purpose of TDD.

Talking with Agile Manifesto authors elicits a range of ideas and opinions. But there is one opinion that is fairly common among us all — that people and organizations have focused far too much on *doing* Agile and far too little on *being* Agile. Many organizations have failed to reap the benefits of Agile, or even to recoup their investment, because they adopted the practices without the mind-set — creating a discordance that couldn't be overcome.

Gil's book will help overcome this discordance, either by defining an Agile mind-set and showing you how to apply it, or by cautioning why Agile may not be a good fit in your culture.

Jim Highsmith
Executive Consultant, ThoughtWorks
Lafayette, Colorado

FOREWORD

by Linda Rising

This readable, insightful book examines the values, beliefs, and principles supporting Agile thinking. If I were brainstorming alternative titles I might suggest: *Thinking about Agile Thinking*.

I find that so much of what's captured here mirrors my own cognitive struggles. Not only thinking about thinking (I have been talking about my interpretation of the "Agile mind-set" since 2011) but, since the creation of the Agile Manifesto in 2001, thinking about the contributions of that document: the idea that we could talk about values in software development. The idea that we could focus on the people who participate in software development. The idea that values could lead to decision-enhancing principles. These revelations have enabled this industry to have wider impact. Everything has changed because of Agile.

Gil Broza's book has given us a framework for lifting up those values, beliefs, and principles and shaking out the tangled connections that we've been making since 2001. The web we have woven over the past decade has sometimes led us to confused implementations and struggles that have caused many to blame Agile, when it's our own slow understanding of the big picture that is at fault. We saw Agile as a collection of band-aids and we have attempted to select the ones with our favorite cartoon characters to patch the most obvious sore places. We, the walking wounded, have been helped in some cases, but in others we only made things worse. We failed to get the message about a new way of thinking, not realizing that it was more than just some new steps in the dance to produce products.

This book is full of stories. I love stories. We all love to hear what others who face similar problems have done. It makes everything in the book seem "more real" and easier to apply. Gil invited some of his clients and colleagues to share their point of view; that always adds credibility and helps us get a sense that others, just like us, have valuable lessons learned and are generously willing to share. I appreciate that.

Many of the stories are about the obvious. Why not just ask for help when you need it? Why not just explain how we work when someone seems confused or misunderstands what you are doing? These stories carry a profound message, building on the assumption that most people we encounter in our business are smart, work hard, and want to do a good job. Not a bad way to proceed, and, most of the time, very effective. Lots of patterns here!

Since I give a talk about deception and estimation, I especially enjoyed the interesting estimation exercise and the story about estimating a house move. No spoiler here; you'll have to read it for yourself! I love the estimation heuristics.

I like Gil's proposal that YAGNI is better replaced with "you don't need it now," which is not so much of a blow to the ego of the proposer and doesn't close the door on future opportunities. It almost seems counterintuitive, given the emphasis on the "here and now" benefit bias, to say, "It's okay sometimes to think about the future!"

I know you have your own favorite Agile hot button, and I know you'll enjoy reading Gil's insights on whatever that issue might be. I believe we'll all get better and better as a result of his starting this conversation. It's time we all started thinking about Agile thinking.

Linda Rising
Coauthor, Fearless Change *and* More Fearless Change
Nashville, Tennessee

INTRODUCTION

When you think about "Agile" (or "agile"), what noun follows it?

Many people talk about Agile development, Agile project management, Agile processes, Agile methods, and Agile best practices. Some speak about the Agile Methodology or the Agile Framework. Others refer to pairings like Scrum/Agile and Lean/Agile. There is capital-A Agile and small-a agile. Confused already?

Agile — capital-A Agile — is a particular way of working, often useful when the work is complex, changing, or uncertain. As such, it's more than process and methods. So what is it? To some people, the word "methodology" conjures images of thick rule books. If you say, "Agile development," the common association is with software. If you say, "Agile project management," many software people may start arguing with you.

So what word best comes after "Agile"? My way out of this bind is to just say, "Agile," with no word after it. (Lean[1] practitioners get out of their own arguments the same way.) This enables me to apply Agile *thinking* to various types of product development, to complex projects, to my business, and even to raising my kids. If I'm pressed to find a more serious-sounding word for *thinking*, I'll use "paradigm" or "mind-set."

This is important, because Agile transcends process, practices, and technique, and applies to people and product as well. When you operate with an Agile mind-set, it permeates everything you do and say. Moreover, it's a whole package. To achieve its benefits — which in product development include happy customers, quality product, solid teams, and faster results — you cannot cherry-pick which of its values and principles you like; you have to embrace all of them.

Take *early and frequent value delivery*, for instance. Clearly, this business promise requires appropriate process and planning elements. Those elements must be *adaptive*, because the meaning of value changes over time and context. Thus, small time-boxes (iterations) and flow are suitable options for managing work, whereas a staged or sequential model with early commitment is not. As well, *putting people first* is critical for those in delivery roles to *collaborate with their customer* in a trusting relationship that enables both of them to adapt. If the product is software, the development team must use adaptive techniques to build, test, and deploy the software quickly and safely; prolonged manual testing is not a suitable option.

These days, more and more senior managers pursue cheaper, better, and faster results. Especially in product development, a tempting option is available: switch to using Agile methods. All too often, though, they adopt visible elements of Agile, but not its mind-set. For instance:

- ✦ They have backlogs, but their backlog items are not simple; they are detailed specifications.

- ✦ Their team members don't collaborate (or care for collaboration); each person just works on their own tasks.

- ✦ Rather than assiduously seeking and applying feedback, they limit it to prescribed meetings.

- ✦ Instead of embracing servant leadership, they focus on task management and policing the team's adherence to the process.

In too many cases, the results are mediocre (or worse), and the implementers and practitioners can't explain why. One reason I've written this book is to give them insights beyond process and "best practices" so they may make better choices and improve their situation. While there is no singular recipe for Agile to succeed, this book will show you what ingredients you, as an Agile chef, would need for your recipe, as well as how to combine these ingredients for your success.

My second reason for writing the book is that even when organizations and managers intend to start their Agile journey with the right mind-set, many don't realize the magnitude and complexity of the transformation. Along the way, they cause unintended casualties, lose their staff's trust, and do shoddy work. In many organizations, a proper move to Agile would be nothing short of a revolution (ideally, the revolutionaries would all agree on what the new regime should be like). In fact, in some places the Agile transformation looks just like a revolution, with its share of ideologists, purists, visionaries, heretics, casualties, and mavericks. That's too bad, because there's nothing about Agile that calls for ideology; it's merely a way of approaching certain types of work (and Agile intends to draw people closer, not apart!). Without choosing sides or attaching to a specific process, this book will help you see beyond mechanics and ideology, so that your Agile journey can be better informed.

The third reason for the book is to give readers an unbiased, accurate picture of the Agile thought process. Having been a practitioner, manager, facilitator, coach, trainer, speaker, and consultant since its early days (2001), I've seen it evolve mightily. I've witnessed all the positives and negatives of a movement being born and coming of age. While my background and specialty are in software development, I've seen Agile thinking applied to many other disciplines. Through all this, I've witnessed the amazing benefits that accrue with a true Agile mind-set, and I've met people who never realized those benefits because they'd written Agile off for the wrong reasons (a popular one being "too many meetings!"). This book will help you reflect more deeply and accurately on the Agile paradigm so you can make an informed opinion about it — including when *not* to use it.

The first chapter of this book gives the big picture of the Agile mind-set. The next seven chapters show what the mind-set says specifically about these aspects of work:

◆ Deciding what to work on

◆ Planning the work

◆ Engaging people

◆ Performing as a team

◆ Doing the work (in any Agile setting *and* more specifically in software development)

◆ Getting better at work

The last chapter explains how individuals and organizations can effectively adopt the mind-set.

The dozens of stories you'll read are all true. Most are from teams I've coached or observed, while a few have been contributed by clients, reviewers, and colleagues.

Most chapters come with free resources, such as checklists, worksheets, and cheat sheets. Download these resources from the book's companion website at www.TheAgileMindsetBook.info.

One of my principles in writing this book was to structure it for quick and easy consumption. Another one was to provoke your thinking about Agile and take it to the next level. That is why the book is not shorter. Still, if you only have time for two chapters, read the bookends: chapters 1 and 9; you will learn *about* the mind-set. However, if you'd like to *know the mind-set* so you get better results from Agile, read chapters 1–9 in order.

You won't find dogma in this book. You won't find preference for any Agile process framework over another. Nor will you receive any prescription of practices, processes, or tools, since they won't take account of your unique situation. Instead, you will get a multifaceted exploration of the way many people like to think and operate as they tackle the needs and challenges of modern knowledge work.

Chapter 1
The Big Picture

Your mind-set is how you think about acting in a given situation. The object of your mind-set can be anything that draws a response from you: work, parenting, health, self-development, community, politics, and other aspects of your life. You choose that particular mind-set, as opposed to others, to maximize the chances of achieving your objectives and meeting your needs in the situation.

Whether you choose your mind-set deliberately or unawares; whether it's appropriate for your objectives or not; whether it's static or varies with context; whether it's universal or uniquely yours — *it's the thinking that drives your actions.* This book focuses on the Agile mind-set, a specific approach to certain kinds of work.

1

This chapter describes the elements of a mind-set and tells how it affects process, decisions, and actions. It then draws the big picture of the Agile mind-set and its applicability, leaving the details and specifics to the rest of the book.

Elements of a Mind-Set

I've found it useful to consider mind-set as having three elements:

1. **Values**: What you consider most important in the current situation

2. **Beliefs**: What you hold to be true in that type of situation

3. **Principles**: Which standards guide your choices, decisions, and actions

In a given work situation, you will value some things higher than others, and you will make assumptions about the work and the people involved in it. Based on those values and beliefs, you will embrace a set of principles for approaching the work. Those principles will describe:

+ How to make the work count,

+ How to support the work's objectives,

+ Which variables to manage as the work progresses, and

+ The human environment in which all this takes place.

As an example, here is a partial snapshot of my mind-set in writing this book. It's particularly important to me that readers can process it easily, and actually use it to improve their Agility. I believe that too many practitioners focus too much on process, practices, and techniques. I believe that so little has been written about the Agile mind-set that practitioners struggle to explain it to others and to themselves. I believe my readers would prefer an impartial book, which helps them think through Agile for themselves without my "selling" it to them. Therefore, my writing principles include: write

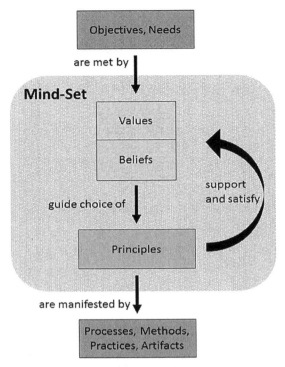

conversationally, keep it simple, provoke thoughts, open readers' minds, tell stories, and don't take sides.

The sum total of values, beliefs, and principles is your mind-set about the work at hand. Determining it, however, is just the beginning. The next step is to choose or design processes, practices, methods, and tools — all the visible parts of work that yield results. Backed by the mind-set, these parts will guide you in deciding what to work on, how to plan, how to do the work, how to engage people and teams, and how to work better.

Even if you consciously adopt an explicit mind-set, you might not feel confident designing useful processes and practices. Most people are simply not used to doing that, nor necessarily cognizant of the ramifications of certain choices. If your situation involves industry, production, development, or operations, you have a shortcut: adopt established mind-sets — complete "packages" of values, beliefs, and principles — that others have found to be generally useful. Here are a few popular examples:

✦ If you care most about collaborating with your customers, delighting them frequently, responding to change if it's worth responding to, and doing all this in an environment where workers can thrive together, you might choose the Agile mind-set.

✦ If you consider that getting the solution right the first time and maximizing predictability are the most important drivers, then the Waterfall mind-set might appeal to you.

✦ If your business objectives require you to manufacture many copies of the same product, to allow some customer-specific variations, and to keep your inventory low, you might consider the Lean Production mind-set promising.

✦ If your top need is to convince yourself that your solution is right for the problem *and that you're solving the right problem*, the Lean Startup mind-set might be the right fit.

The key point is that before you ever plan, commit, design, implement, improve, or otherwise *do* work in a given situation, you should be clear on your objectives and be explicit and deliberate about your mind-set. You do that by identifying your most important values, eliciting your beliefs about the work, and choosing principles to guide and govern your actions. *Doing so is neither quick nor easy.* You may have little experience in the matter. Or, you may assume that you have no influence over the approach. And if you feel inclined to reuse a mind-set that has served you before, be aware that you might be trading the effective for the expedient and comfortable.

For two examples of this mindful approach to work, see "Mindful Process Design" in appendix B.

Agile Values

My clients are organizations that spend considerable time and money on product development. In early conversations with me, they will usually express the reasons or objectives for their work: increase market share, automate a business process, strengthen a brand, reduce operational expenses, and so on. I like to follow this up with a specific question:

"What is important to you in your work?"

If you're like most people, your answer would include a few dozen items and take you several minutes to produce. You would then need a bit longer to sort your list such that the *most important* ones are on top and in the right order for you. If you're in a group of people responsible for the work, this task may take even longer.

Examples of commonly held values around work (not held all at the same time) are:

- ✦ Minimize cost and schedule
- ✦ Build the right thing
- ✦ Make accurate commitments
- ✦ Eliminate the risk of disaster
- ✦ Maximize perceived quality
- ✦ Be able to change priorities quickly
- ✦ Be able to replace the workers easily
- ✦ Innovate
- ✦ Keep auditors happy
- ✦ Build happy teams that work well together
- ✦ Get rewarded or promoted

Agile is anchored in four foundational values — meaning, if you choose the Agile approach for the work at hand, your top-ranked values include (and don't contradict) the Agile four:

People come first, before product and before process. Those people are everyone with a stake in the work, not just the team that produces it; customers and managers are people too. This value is known in the Agile community as "individuals and interactions."

Adaptation. Opportunities and need for change — of mind, of understanding, or of circumstance — will occur; embrace those changes that are worth embracing (e.g., for competitive advantage). Adaptation encompasses the readiness, ability, and willingness to respond to change. The change may apply to people, process, or product.

Early and frequent value delivery. The work has some customer, perhaps even several. They might be paying, or not, and they might not be the end users. The workers ought to focus relentlessly on doing valuable work and making a difference, so their customers see an early and frequent return on investment.*

Customer collaboration. The producers of the work ought to collaborate with their customers for the result to truly delight them. It is a spirit of partnership, not of vendor-buyer or winner-loser.

It's certainly possible, even likely, to espouse a wider set of values than these in a given situation. For example, Agile practitioners often need to control their costs and put contracts in place. Agile may be a good fit, however, when its four values *matter more* than the other ones.

[*Historical note:* The term "Agile" dates back to February 2001, when 17 software development professionals and thought leaders who had experimented with "lightweight" methods met to identify their common ground. They coined the term "Agile software development" and penned "The Agile Manifesto."[1] Given their common goal — and disenchantment with prevailing methods of software development — one of the Manifesto's four values is "working soft-

---

*   Note that the word "value" has two close but different meanings. As a countable noun (e.g., "the four Agile values"), it means "important thing." As an uncountable noun (e.g., "customer value") it means "worth," particularly in exchange for something.

ware." Over time, they and other thought leaders have expanded Agile thinking to domains that had similar challenges to software development. In this generalized form, "working software" has turned to "early and frequent value delivery." The other three values have stayed unchanged.]

Agile Beliefs

When you picked up a book titled *The Agile Mind-Set*, you probably didn't expect it to bring up the matter of *beliefs*. Beliefs conjure religious associations, but in the context of the Agile mind-set, they mean anything but.

A belief is a conviction. It's something you hold to be true but haven't proven, and perhaps can't prove rigorously. As such, beliefs are harder to shift than assumptions. Beliefs help you make sense of your environment and of how to do well in it. In a work context, common beliefs include:

+ Placing workers where their skills are most needed is a good way to finish projects.

+ If we propose a compelling, sensible improvement, people will naturally want to implement it, and proceed to do that.

+ People really care only for themselves.

+ If we do all the design before starting implementation, we reduce risk and avoid rework.

+ The documentation of how a piece is constructed will be useful to the next team member on the job.

+ If we invite certain senior managers to our meetings, we won't get in trouble later.

+ If we hire great people, we'll have great performance.

✦ If we sign off on requirements now and the team will finish developing them six months from now, the requirements will still be valuable and relevant.

Beliefs are invisible and often hard to articulate. And, their effect on choices cannot be understated. Consider for example that popular value in business, "Be the leader in our market." A business that pursues it, and believes that its customers care most about service, might base its operations on the principle of giving customers a great experience. Another business in the same segment could also want to be the leader, but believe instead that customers care mostly about price; it might organize its work to minimize the customer's cost. While values do not uniquely determine beliefs, they make certain beliefs relevant and others irrelevant or improbable.

Agile has a set of beliefs about people, the work, and the work's customer.

People. The Agile mind-set is congruent with Theory Y, which says that competent, motivated, trusted, and supported people will do well.[2] Pragmatically, though — the Agile thinking goes — as human beings they will get some (or even many) things wrong. Even when they're right, they're not perfect, but working closely together enriches the outcomes that they could achieve individually. In light of the four values, people with an Agile mind-set believe that the best model that manages the downside and elevates the upside is the self-organizing, collaborative team.

The customer. Two of the Agile values are focused on the customer — the entity that wants the results of the work (the two other values, a little less so). However, the Agile mind-set does not assume that the customer is always right. In fact, its basic belief is that customers can't — and, being adaptive, shouldn't — pinpoint future needs and wants. Moreover, even if they have a good handle on what's needed *now*, delaying implementation will make those requirements go stale. The sensible thing to do, therefore, is to focus intently on what the customer needs now, and not commit too far into the future. Knowing the top needs and fulfilling them is being effective, which from an Agile standpoint matters more than being efficient.

The work. Even if the four Agile values are indeed your most important values, and even if you agree with the beliefs mentioned so far, what is true of the work? The Agile mind-set is formulated particularly for *complex* work.[3] As such, it's based on a particular belief: *emergence*, or *evolution* — rather than planning — is an appropriate response to complexity. And what's the best enabler of emergence? The short feedback loop. Since feedback, emergence, and adaptation imply frequent change, a key Agile assumption is that the cost of change *can remain low*. When this isn't the case — for instance in some civil engineering projects — Agile will probably not be a good fit.

It bears repeating that all the abovementioned statements are only *beliefs*. They cannot be proven the way mathematical laws can. Agile practitioners adhere to these beliefs — and use them to justify their choice of principles — because they see enough compelling evidence for their validity.

Agile Principles

The third element in a work mind-set, principles, describes how work gets done. Practitioners use the principles to design their methods and processes.*

---

* Throughout the book (and particularly in this chapter), I consistently distinguish between values, beliefs, and principles based on the definitions presented earlier. I've found this distinction to be useful for having emotionally neutral conversations about Agile and even more so about the adoption of the mind-set. If you've learned about Agile from other sources, you might have seen them use the terms differently or interchangeably.

When people formulate a mind-set, they choose its principles to support their values and beliefs. It might include any number of principles; Agile has 26 (sorry, there really is a lot to it!).* As we examine the principles throughout the book, we'll keep referring back to the values and beliefs that justify them.

It's important to note that a set of values and beliefs doesn't give rise to a single possible set of principles. Take for instance the desire to deliver value to the customer early and frequently. You might decide to support it with a single principle: "Complete and deliver one customer-valued item at a time." Or you could pick another principle: "Whenever the client makes a request, drop everything and address what they want right now." The Agile mind-set happens to accomplish the value with several other principles, whose (short) names are Cadence, Reliability, Simplicity, Shippable, Quality, Time-Box, and Collaboration. We examine these and the other Agile principles in the rest of this section. (Wherever the short name for a principle appears, it will be **in boldface**.)

Principles Regarding People

Did you notice that the first of the four Agile values is not about work, but about the workers? The early Agile thought leaders — who first made the mind-set explicit in the context of software development — asserted that while processes and tools are important, the *individuals* and their *interactions* matter more. In fact,

---

* The Agile Manifesto lists only 12 principles, most of which it frames in the context of software development. Since its writing in 2001, countless organizations and thought leaders have applied those principles and generalized them to nonsoftware pursuits. They have also incorporated ideas from other paradigms. Through experimentation and introspection, the Agile community seems to have reached consensus on a total of 26 principles that support the Agile values and beliefs (see note 4). This book might be the first to present them as such.

they deliberately made that the first value statement in the Agile Manifesto. This assertion has given rise to a comprehensive set of principles regarding people.

First, the *"individuals"* part. Agile environments are built on **respect, transparency, trust**, and **personal safety**. These conditions enable people to participate; beyond that, people will do their best work if they can **focus** and work at a **sustainable pace**.

Second, the *"interactions"* part. In Agile, the people who transform ideas into delivered value organize themselves in teams. And not just any teams, but cross-functional, semiautonomous, and **self-organizing** ones. In plain language, their members have the necessary skills and abilities to complete valuable work, are empowered to make many of the "how" decisions, and determine which member will do what when. And even that is only half the story!

Where possible and relevant, an Agile team is also **collaborative**: members work together and share ownership over their results. This is quite distinct from traditional environments, where people might be helpful and cooperative, but default to working on their own tasks. Agile teams establish maximum-bandwidth means of **communication** so everyone stays informed. When they make decisions, their preferred mode is to achieve **consensus**: to gain everyone's support for the decisions' implementation, even if not everybody is wild about them.

The Agile team model is flatter and more self-managing than most organizations are used to. To facilitate their growth and integration into the organization, Agile promotes **leadership**. Specifically, it calls for having servant leaders who grow teams in a trusting, supportive, and humane environment.

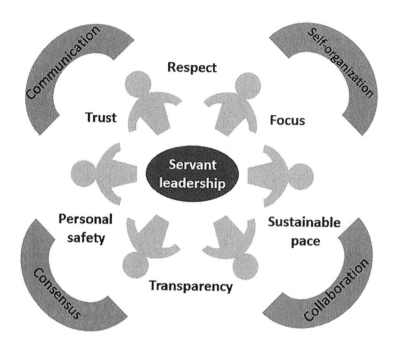

The Agile principles regarding people
("Individuals and interactions")

Principles Regarding Work

As noted earlier, a mind-set about work also has principles to describe how to make the work count, how to support objectives, and which variables to manage as the work progresses.

Making the work count. Every activity in Agile starts by understanding its **outcome** or objective. This is also known as "begin with the end in mind."[5] If you need to choose between being effective (doing the right thing) and being efficient (minimizing waste), prefer to be **effective**. Put another way, always ask "Why?" before you ask "What?" and only then be concerned with the "How?"

Three additional principles help you achieve more of the right outcomes and produce fewer of the wrong ones. First, **defer** decisions to the last responsible moment: don't make commitments earlier than you have to. Wait as long as you can to make a better-informed decision without incurring too much risk. Second, when determining outcomes, making decisions, and doing work, strive for **simplicity**. And third, when certainty is unjustified, take an **experimental** approach: fail fast and cheap, and maximize the learning from that.

Supporting objectives. The Agile mind-set views such objectives through the lens of customer and business value. The **cadence** principle tells the team to deliver value as frequently as desirable and possible, from both a technical and a business perspective. The team does that with **reliability**, ensuring they do not compromise their future ability to deliver value. Put another way, they avoid quick, dirty, "just-get-it-out" implementations, because of the long-term impact on value delivery. And to satisfy the adaptation expectation — tomorrow's objectives may not be the same as today's — a third principle is needed: organize the work and the team to reduce the **cost of change**, not the cost of work. Consider where the product is likely to change in the future, and keep options open for that.

The variables to manage as the work proceeds. The Agile team's guideline for progress is to keep their product in a working, **shippable**, and preferably deployed state. Why? Because keeping it this way means the team is never far from the next opportunity for value delivery. Seeing progress this way, as something the team is collectively responsible for, gives rise to another principle: the team's **results** matter more than the members' individual utilization. In Agile, delighting the customer is more important than keeping everyone maximally busy.

Quality is a factor of value. When it's low, it doesn't just reduce value; it hampers work. To enable regular progress, Agile practitioners pay constant attention to **quality** and technical excellence.

In terms of the other common constraints around work — time, scope, and cost — Agile's preference is for time; the **time-box** governs much of Agile planning.

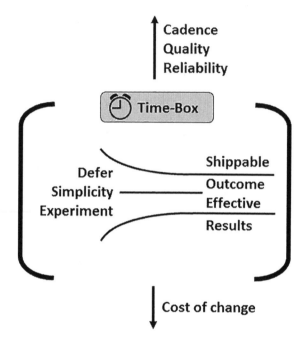

The Agile principles regarding work

Meta-Principles

Three additional principles enhance and modulate the ones described above. The first is to incorporate **feedback** loops into everything, and make them short and actionable. After all, feedback enables change and adaptation. The second is continual **learning** about things that constantly shift: the customers, the business, the team, and the work. Building on the first two, the third principle is continuous **improvement**: always do and be better. Process and teamwork improvements are welcome anytime, whereas product improvements are welcome *almost* anytime.

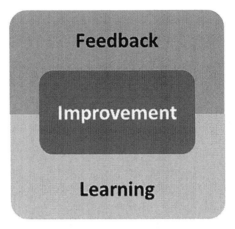

The Agile meta-principles

SUPPLEMENTARY RESOURCE: Download "The Agile Principles" Quick Reference from the book's companion website, **www.TheAgileMindsetBook.info**.

When Is Agile a Good Fit?

Traveling in certain circles, you'll get the impression that Waterfall is obsolete and harmful, and Agile is the One Sensible Way to go. The truth is that each approach has its strengths and weaknesses, and situations it fits well. An organization (and a person) may benefit from the Agile paradigm in some lines of work, and from a more plan-driven and efficiency-minded paradigm in others.

To determine which paradigm suits your work situation, start by identifying what is important to you given your objectives. In other words, what are your top values around this particular work? For example, do you want to minimize your expenditure? Be ready to change course if a competitor disrupts your market? Guarantee certain schedule milestones? Develop your team? Spread out the return on investment by delivering frequently? If several aspects are important to you, which ones matter the most to you *now*?

Your answers will differ by context and by product. If you're creating a textbook, an office chair, a movie, yoga pants, a Web application, or a mobile phone, expect different answers. If you're creating the next generation of an existing product, your answers now and back then may be different. Once you identify your values, do they mostly overlap with the Agile set, the Waterfall one, or something else? (To read my analysis of the Waterfall values, beliefs, and principles and how they compare to Agile, see appendix A.)

Let's assume that the values guide your attention to Agile. You're not done yet; the Agile principles will matter, and will yield the desired benefits, only if the Agile beliefs apply in your situation. If you, your team, and your organization see things differently — for instance, you believe it's possible and desirable to predetermine all the major tasks — the principles alone will not help, and may even backfire.

The following checklists recast the foundational values, beliefs, and principles as questions to determine Agile's fit to your situation. As you consider your answers to the questions, make sure you're being honest with yourself.

The people:

+ Do your people feel safe and trusted? (In particular, does the culture tolerate making mistakes, and do people have safety nets?)

+ Will the organization welcome a high level of transparency?

+ Will the organization allow a collaborative, self-organizing, cross-functional team to grow and thrive?

+ Are quick, actionable feedback loops possible?

+ Will the team be able to dedicate time to learning and improvement?

The customer:

✦ Can the team establish a relationship with their customer that is collaborative and involves frequent interaction?

✦ Can the customer generally choose and articulate the top needs in a timely and reliable fashion?

✦ Will the customer tolerate some uncertainty about cost, scope, and schedule in return for adaptation and frequent value delivery?

✦ Does the customer prefer the discovery of valuable alternatives over the efficient execution of a predetermined solution?

The work:

✦ Are you solving an important problem, and do you have a rough idea about a solution worth building?

✦ Is there significant uncertainty (or unjustified certainty) around needs, design, or execution?

✦ Even with good certainty, can you expect opportunities for change to occur later that will be worth seizing?

✦ Does the complexity of the work justify considerable collaboration among team members?

✦ At the time of execution, will information, discoveries, and preferences invalidate many early decisions?

✦ Are you making something you haven't made before? (Put another way, is this a design or development situation rather than a manufacturing or production one?)

✦ Can you keep the cost of change low?

✦ Will people continue to work on the product after it's "done"?

These questions result in "yes" answers across much of software development — both commercial product development and IT — hence Agile's popularity there. However, they also apply to other types of product, knowledge, and design work, so the mind-set may well apply there, too.

For a nonsoftware example, read my personal account of applying the Agile mind-set to home renovations in appendix B.

If you answer "yes" to all the questions, and implement all the principles, you have a good reason to expect the Agile benefits: delighted customers, quality product, reliable and healthy teams, and faster releases. If these checklists seem like a tall order, that's because they are. If they weren't, the world of product development would have been quite nimble by now. After you learn about the mind-set in depth in the next chapters, in chapter 9 you will learn how to adopt the mind-set.

Many elements of the Agile mind-set are neither new nor an invention of Agile pioneers. Its power comes from being taken as a whole — as a coherent, self-reinforcing set of values, beliefs, and principles. In this form, it's been around for almost 20 years, and the world keeps refining it. The following chapters explain how the mind-set addresses the six elements of work:

+ Deciding what to work on

+ Planning the work

+ Engaging people (as opposed to using machines)

+ Performing as a team (as opposed to a group)

+ Doing the work

+ Getting better at work

Chapter 2
Deciding What to Work On

I f you're going to spend your time and energy on some work, that work has to matter. How do you decide what to work on, and how do you know you're right? This chapter explains how the Agile mind-set answers these key questions.

Outcome and Purpose

At my clients, teams tend to work on projects that last several months to a year. During initial assessments and early coaching, I ask every role player: "What does success mean on your project?"

In most cases, the answer is a variation on "Deliver on time and on budget."

I don't know about you, but I fail to find this answer useful, motivating, or interesting. It seems to discount the significance of content (scope), quality, and user experience. It doesn't express why the particular schedule and cost *matter*. And it does nothing to explain why the team is working on this project instead of another. If I follow my question by asking, "Deliver what?" the answer tends to be something like, "the stuff we put in the backlog."

Well, how would you know *what* to put in the backlog, and in what order? What guides your choices?

Stephen Covey has taught the world to adopt a habit called "begin with the end in mind." This is both a principle and a habit in Agile, since it's present in every activity.

I interpret the word "end" in two ways. The first is, what result will you have in the end? What outcome will you produce? The second meaning goes beyond the outcome: To what end? What's the purpose of your next action? *Why* do it?

If your team spends several months developing something, what is the end, purpose, or objective of their work? Implementing solutions is merely the means. My question to uncover the purpose is:

> "How will you make a difference to your
> organization, to the users, to the world?"

I usually need to probe a bit more, so I ask:

> "And why is that difference worth making?"

These simple questions are powerful, and more palatable to the respondents than the blunt short form, "Why are you working on this?" Here are examples of answers from two teams I've coached:

"We'll make our product support 50,000 customers and 5,000,000 visitors in a month. We believe that will allow us both technologically and conceptually to increase our market share to 25%."

"We'll give our analysts a reliable, integrated portfolio research tool that will displace Microsoft Excel."

Discovering the outcome and crystallizing its reasons is rarely easy or fast, especially when you consider large efforts such as in these examples. Yet Agile practitioners apply the same line of thinking to smaller efforts:

- Iteration: "What is our goal for this iteration?"

- Work items: "What will be possible when this item is implemented? What value does it have?"

- Meeting: "What's the purpose of this meeting?"

- Programming: "What's the next little behavior we're building?"

- Testing: "What are we hoping to learn from the next test?"

One reason teams have coaches and leaders is to constantly remind them to ask these questions until they truly become a habit. Unfortunately, many Agile teams develop mediocre products because they don't ask the questions frequently enough. The most impactful failure is when they start their projects by filling up a backlog and jumping into their first iteration, never having distilled what their work is about and why they're doing it.

Agile practitioners like to answer these questions collaboratively, typically in facilitated meetings. They also like to revisit their answers regularly. Both approaches create shared understanding and reduce mistakes. Unfortunately, it's still common for senior managers to envision projects and for product owners to articulate requirements without involving the team and extended project community members. I know of one case in which incorporating this diversity turned a hardware project "with a bit of programming" into an 18-month software project "with some firmware and hardware." Even without such an extreme surprise, keeping the end in mind helps you decide what to work on and, more importantly, what *not* to work on.

Customer

Business analysts, user experience designers, marketing managers, product managers — for many years, technology development staff included people like these with the necessary skills and disciplines to determine what specifically to build and for whom. Then Extreme Programming (XP) came along, recommending that the customer work closely and interact continuously with the delivery team. This way, the team and the customer would build shared understanding, catch mistakes, allow changes early, and focus their efforts on what the customer actually needs.

This idea caught on only partially. For one thing, those customers' day jobs haven't gone away entirely. For another, what if there are multiple customers? Who has a say? What if some of the customers are senior managers? What if the customer is the general public, or people the team has no access to (such as employees at another corporation)? What if the people who evaluate the team's product are not its eventual users?

The most popular solution is to interact with users as much as possible, but still have someone play the role of "product owner." Acting as a representative of the sponsors, stakeholders, and users, the product owner reconciles their different voices into a single voice for the delivery team to hear. The principle at play is focus: have the team work from a single list. The product owner has the organizational

One program team I've coached was developing a hub for data from dozens of source systems. Due to complex upstream and downstream dependencies, the concept of a single product owner didn't work for them. Instead, a prioritization committee of four leads determined the sequence of source systems and handling of change requests. Two of the members were senior, but the committee preferred to rely on majority consensus: binding decisions would pass if at least three members agreed.

sanction to populate, order, and change the list — preferably, in collaboration with the team and after reaching consensus.

In most Agile environments, the team learns what to do from someone who is not their boss. At least in technology, teams seem to respond differently to this situation than to the traditional one, in which they simply execute on their manager's plans. They ask "Why" and push back a lot more, which results in more creative and less unnecessary work. They also strengthen their ties to "the business" and improve their understanding of it. In some organizations that have adopted the Agile mind-set, technology and business have transitioned from adversaries to partners.

Since the product owner has the ultimate responsibility to determine what to work on, the role can't be staffed by just anyone. The product owner must be empowered, knowledgeable, and available. If he or she can't make hard decisions, doesn't know enough, or can't interact with the team enough, someone else will have to make up the shortfall. The results are rarely satisfactory. If your team can't have a product owner who fulfills these requirements, several of the

In most cases, a technology team will work directly with a single product owner who represents the business side of the organization. Your context, however, might not fit the standard mold. Here are examples from my experience and my colleagues':

+ On one team that upgraded a product's database to its vendor's next generation, the product owner was a systems architect.

+ On another team, no single person could fit the product owner profile because of the complex nature of the domain and individual availability. Instead, two business analysts acted as "pair product owners."

+ A team that develops a search engine knows the business so well by now, they govern the search solution on their own, without a product owner.

Agile values and principles will be compromised. Either find another way to implement them, or consider that perhaps Agile is not a good fit for your situation.

Value

Having discovered how their project makes a difference, many teams erroneously move straight to solutioning and task determination. The Agile mind-set, however, prefers to first view the work as a series of items that have explicit or implicit *value*. But what is value?

The vagueness of the term "value" makes it well-chosen, since value is in the eye of the beholder. In one company it could be dollars, and in another it could be retaining customers or increasing word-of-mouth referrals. You might argue that everything boils down to dollars, but that effect can be quite indirect and hard to quantify or even approximate.

It's easiest to think of delivering value to end users, especially if a software or hardware feature is involved: users can do something with the system or product that they couldn't do before. This is "customer value." Customer value sometimes parlays into higher sales and customer retention, which in turn spell value to the organization funding the work: that's "business value."

An organization may realize business value without producing customer value. This can be in the form of lowering expenses or increasing goodwill. Investments also generate business value if they make subsequent work cheaper, easier, or possible. For instance, software development teams that modernize outdated frameworks gain value for their business, even if the end user doesn't notice any change.

One popular type of work item in Agile processes — the user story — typically indicates what someone or something does with the system to obtain a valuable result. However, some work items are all about another subcategory of business value: receiving useful feedback. Prototypes and early-design stories are an example: they result in feedback — technical and otherwise — that helps direct further work. Rather than having monetary value, these stories facilitate work that may lead to money.

Use the customer value and business value lenses to examine everything the organization *needs* and the team *does*. It doesn't matter whether value is direct or indirect, monetary or otherwise. It might flow from features, abilities, and/or user experience. There may be value in doing just enough of something, or by going the extra mile. The important thing is to have a shared understanding of value in *your* context.

Delight

During the kickoff for a project meant to extend a Web portal, a team identified "quality work" as a value. As we were discussing the various definitions of "quality" (e.g., defect-free, fit for purpose), I offered this interpretation: "Quality products *delight* your customers."

This was when the fun started. Some folks were puzzled, others wide-eyed. One of the guys was outright rankled: "I don't want to delight! Why not just satisfy?"

"Well," I said, "do satisfied users come back for more business, or do the delighted ones?"

People then argued with the concept of delight. Why bother? Nobody's trying to delight *them*! "Actually," I said, "all of you know several companies and products that aim to delight you. Can you think of a few?"

Soon enough, the team came up with some examples: Google search, iPhone, Firefox, Photoshop. Slowly, the mood shifted. Within a few minutes, this group of people had found new motivation for their project. The verb "delight" became something of an anchor for the workshop.

The IT professionals in this story truly wanted to do their job well. In their environment, however, doing their job well meant finishing their tasks on time and with acceptable quality. The presumption is that once the team's tasks are determined, they are correct and useful.

But when the team is done, will the customers be delighted, satisfied, neutral, upset, or fuming? This question doesn't even come up.

Agile is grounded in only four values, yet all four play into customer experience. By receiving value early and often, the customer can reach smaller objectives sooner instead of larger objectives later. The team and the customer alike expect to collaborate: to understand which objectives to meet, how, and when, in order to make the biggest difference. If needs change, the team can quickly adapt their plans so the customer doesn't have to wait long. Lastly, Agile's people orientation makes both parties understand each other as human beings, not as abstract consumer-provider entities.

"Delight" may take different forms. If the customer regularly spends hours per week on a cumbersome administrative procedure, a "good enough for now" Web form may bring more joy to them than a slower-to-develop glitzy interface. If an operating system's users were used to navigating to their software programs a certain way and an upgrade took that ability away, reinstating it can make them very happy (or less upset). If a certain technology's users can say, "It just *works*. I can trust it to never break," they may be far more delighted about that than about extra features. Simplicity — one of the Agile principles — guides practitioners to prefer good-enough-for-now solutions over complex ones if they delight the customer sooner. Another Agile principle — reliability — guides their choices away from the shortsighted and throwaway toward those that do not jeopardize their ability to deliver value later.

Although the team in my story chose to go beyond "satisfy," they stopped short of "delight" and settled on "please." Here's how they put it in a sentence: "We believe in quality work, therefore we will respond to the business's needs in order to please our end users, perform each task to the best of our abilities, and be proud of our final product."

Field Testing

Would you like to order the movie *Confessions of a...* on The Movie Network On Demand?

A few years ago, if you wanted to order a movie from my cable provider, the movie list wouldn't tell you the movie's full name. Even the detailed description screen showed the same truncated title on top. The rest of that space went to the station's logo and a very useful picture of popcorn.

I used to have a Nokia cellphone that boasted a fancy music player. I would use it to play long lectures, podcasts, and audio books. Missed a word or a sentence? Out of luck! No rewind feature that I could find. Bored? No fast-forward. Cassette and CD players had those features decades ago, but that phone's software didn't.

On an eight-hour flight from Barcelona to Toronto, I sat in an aisle seat of the bulkhead row. That's airline lingo for "closest to the lavatory." I was shocked to notice that over a sample of 20 minutes, half of the people who wanted to use that little room didn't know how to open the door. Airplane washroom doors have a strange handle: it is designed not to protrude into the aisle, but it doesn't work well for its intended users. Many of them figured it out *eventually*; one person pushed and jabbed and pulled at the so-called handle for 30 seconds until he gave up and walked away.

None of these stories indicate incompetence on part of the products' planners and developers. Rather, they are all about their approach to feedback and learning.

Product owners identify and prioritize all the necessary features and aspects of their products, "functional" and "nonfunctional" alike. Even with the best intention and knowledge, some of these fall flat once a real user lays hands or eyes on them. Frequent iteration using feedback from testers and actual users helps direct development to areas that matter most.

The trouble is, most product owners are very busy. The magnitude of information they must consider when shaping a product is staggering. Even when they are assisted by analysts, their natural focus is likely on market, features, correctness, and user benefits.

The other trouble is, they often don't possess the deeper skills of user experience and interaction design. In most companies, those skills are in low supply. Eventually, many interaction design decisions are made by programmers and engineers, who are not trained in designing for usability, and who don't interact enough with users to get meaningful feedback.

Feedback and learning are two key Agile principles. The most popular practices that manifest them are automated testing and iteration reviews (sometimes referred to as "show and tell" or "showcases"). But these practices tend to check agreement with the expectations people had going in — and most people like to think they're right — rather than discover where they went wrong. Even deploying frequently isn't helpful if you're not set up to receive and process user feedback.

To better decide what to work on, you need to test your ideas with *real people who have real problems in real situations*. Send developers and testers to visit users and customer sites. Use focus groups and early-access testing. Build mechanisms for collecting feedback and tracking usage into your product. All of these tactics carry a price tag that often triggers push-back. If you do mostly internal testing, which largely amounts to satisfying a spec, you're taking risks; make sure you understand them.

"A client had a problem with a form, in which a checkbox was automatically ticked under specific conditions. From our IT side, this was seen as trivial and could hardly be prioritized. When I went to visit the client, she took me into a room with a TV and said: 'Each time that box is checked, something comes up on that TV that indicates a serious problem and we must prioritize it over anything else. It costs us at least $100K each time and no budget is set for that.' Once we realized the cost of that simple checkbox, we fixed it in a matter of a few days, and added real value."

– Dave Jacques, Agile Coach

Experimentation

No matter how good the product owner and the delivery team are, they will get some things wrong. That's normal, and in some well-known cases, successful products evolved out of a fortuitous discovery while building something else. But when the players *expect* to be wrong sometimes — and not due to incompetence — an interesting shift takes place.

If your team is like most, you probably use a product backlog for the prioritized list of items you plan to get to: items you think you should build. Yet what if you're not sure about some of them? Or you're sure about them, but have a nagging feeling that perhaps you're too confident? If you open your mind to this possibility, would it perhaps behoove you to consider some experiments instead? What if some later items went away if your experiments prove you wrong? Imagine how much time and energy you'd save by *not* doing them!

The bold next step is to deliberately set yourself up to fail usefully on your way to a successful outcome. Instead of presuming that failure is bad, have a system for trying out ideas, use tactics that are supposed to cause failure, and learn from your experiments. (In other words, apply the scientific method.) Two familiar disciplines, usability and test-driven development, embrace failure as a source of learning and valuable design.

Agile practitioners typically use experiments to prove out the value of a solution, especially if it carries a high price tag. To do so, they'll consider simpler, cheaper solutions. For instance, before designing the activities and material for a new open-enrollment workshop, I might run its list of topics by my clients. In another example, a team I used to lead developed software to manage workflows and data in a high-throughput biology company. One of the lab managers asked us one day for a feature to handle a certain form of data correction. We asked his team members to come to us when they needed such a correction, and we'd do it for them manually. Two months later, they'd only asked for it once, so we removed the feature from the backlog and promised to continue manual corrections if necessary.

Agilists like to refer to experimentation as "fail fast, fail cheap, and fail early." Most businesspeople I know twitch a bit when they hear the word "fail." "Learning" and "experimentation" seem to curry a bit more favor, but these terms will meet skepticism and resistance from people who value getting it right the first time (a Waterfall value that's in direct contradiction to Agile).

Organizations and teams have considerable trouble implementing this principle. From a mind-set perspective, if controlling schedule and cost is still of high importance, an experiment looks like a waste of time and money. Moreover, knowledge workers are usually expected to be smart self-starters, so why would they need experiments? And as if that's not enough, there's a reputation problem: experimentation, failing, and trying stuff out seem to reinforce a perception that Agile teams can't be bothered to make commitments. Nevertheless, if an organization is to benefit from Agile, the mind-set must permeate its actions so that failing quickly, cheaply, and early is a normal course of action. This requires a high level of trust.

Feedback

Do you ever get asked to do something, and when you show your results the response is something like, "That's not what I meant"?

Do you sometimes pour your heart and soul into an amazing idea you've had, only to discover people don't even understand what you're talking about?

Agile thinking came about in the mid-1990s as a response to the troubling success rate in software development. Across the industry, many features went unused and entire products fell flat. How could intelligent, well-meaning professionals produce such grim results?

The answer to that was relatively simple: their methods didn't allow for timely, actionable feedback. Core beliefs in the reigning methodology of the time, Waterfall, were that users know what they want and need, you can get that information usefully out of their heads, and it will remain relevant once you're ready with the solution. That might be true for constructing the Golden Gate Bridge, but not in many development situations.

A central principle of the Agile mind-set is to have short, actionable feedback loops, and then to tighten them over time. How do Agile teams typically implement this principle? Work closely with your customer, so you don't discover too late that the fruit of your labor misses the mark. Test every change forthwith to avoid nasty surprises. Demo constructed pieces of the product to your stakeholders, so they can give feedback on the built instead of the imagined. Have teammates give each other feedback on their working relationship and their process, so they can fix problems before they escalate.

So feedback is A Good Thing. Build feedback loops into your process, and your chances of delivering the wrong thing will drop. Now for the bad news: asking for feedback is like going to the doctor.

I always have some development activity on the go: workshops, webinars, events, books. My knowledgeable and patient friend Ted in California often has insightful feedback for me. Before opening registration for my first virtual training, *Individuals and Interactions* (IndividualsAndInteractions.com), I asked Ted for his feedback about the signup page.

You should have heard me groan when I saw his response. It was longer than any feedback he'd ever given me, and it meant hours of extra work I desperately hoped not to have to do. I was conflicted between thinking "Surely what I did isn't so bad" and "His feedback about *The Human Side of Agile* was so useful, why should this be different? Listen to him!"

So I buckled down and did the work (in a slightly foul mood). I actually loved the result. Ted, not as much.... So we went through another cycle. Do you know the feeling of working on something for longer than it "should" take, and you just can't look at it anymore? That's what I felt.

So how, you're wondering, is asking for feedback like going to the doctor? Sometimes, you have to do it, and it's good for you. It costs you time and possibly money. It involves considerable teeth-gnashing (especially during the wait), and you might not like what you hear. What the doctor tells you is not always helpful, practical, empathetic, relevant, or even correct. And another doctor might diagnose and recommend differently....

To make matters worse, you *have to do something* with that feedback. You have to feel safe enough, and have enough self-esteem, to act on feedback that means that some of your work was wrong or wasted. You have to overcome fatigue, procrastination, self-doubt, anger, and a host of human cognitive biases. And once you do the work, you probably need to get it reviewed again. Aargh!

Feedback isn't a new concept. In traditional project management life cycles like Waterfall you also get feedback on your work, usually from internal testing (QA) or user testing (UAT). That feedback often comes late, which isn't great for effective product development, but — and here's the kicker — it's emotionally easier. Having built the thing, you've had your sense of accomplishment. Your mind has rested from that piece of work. You can now deal with needed changes.

Cue Agile, and that sense of accomplishment will feel elusive (or merely delayed). Presumably, it should kick in when the definition of "Done" says it should, not just when you're finished wrapping up your own specialized activity. Yet most of us are not that rational. We should know when we've done well, so we like to apply ourselves, do our bit, declare victory...and move on!

If your Agile implementation feels less than effective, it may well be due to missing or ineffective feedback loops. If that's the case, you have several recourses to choose from:

- ✦ Work in smaller batches: move smaller pieces from idea to production. That immediately translates into shorter feedback loops and fewer comments. And if the feedback amounts to "do it over," your sunk costs are low.

- ✦ Have the entire team establish and process those feedback loops. When people pool their energy and support each other toward a shared vision, they can overcome individual reluctance and procrastination. (To continue the going-to-the-doctor analogy, married people are more likely than unmarried ones to have preventative health checks across a range of conditions.[1] That's getting feedback!)

- ✦ Increase transparency. When information isn't just accessible in theory but also visible — especially information that drives decisions — people are more likely to comment on it.

- ✦ Vary your methods for receiving feedback. For instance, ask both general and specific open-ended questions. Approach people you don't regularly interact with. Observe people's reactions to your product without asking them anything. And if your review meetings with customers and stakeholders yield little or superficial feedback, change the process or format to increase engagement. Be creative!

- ✦ Ask "why" and "what" more often than you ask "how." Rather than be trapped by task lists, keep clear on the purpose of your work and its success criteria. Examples of popular practices that reinforce this advice are writing user stories and acceptance test-driven development (ATDD).

On a personal, human level, when you seek feedback frequently enough, it becomes a habit. When your mind accumulates enough evidence of the value of feedback, it starts wanting more. And if sometimes that translates into "aargh!" and a disheartening pile of work, rely on other people's energy. Seek their encouragement; chat about fun stuff; complain on Twitter. Agile is a team sport; you're not alone.

At the Agile 2009 conference in Chicago, I came across a designer for a software program I used a fair bit. "After a year of using your software," I said, "I have so much feedback for you! I'd love to show you where it's easy, where I'm struggling, and where I'm forced to devise workarounds."

It wasn't the best time, since he had a flight to catch. I was so excited to help — his company had recently adopted Agile. Surely they would be open to feedback and use it wisely! A few days later he followed up to say he was still interested in the feedback. Wonderful! When I suggested a phone call, his brief reply was this:

"If you have feedback on the software from the user's perspective, I'd be happy to receive that via email. If you like, I'll also add your contact information into our new database of users who are interested in participating in testing sessions."

With the first sentence, he just lost me as a potential source of feedback. With the second, he basically said, "and we'll be happy to treat you as telemarketers would!"

I'm sure he's a busy guy. He's an interface designer — probably one of only a few in his company. Still: he designs *how the software is used*. By people. Like me! I practically fell on him out of the blue, offering my time and attention. Responding to this opportunity with "Put it in an email" is wrong on so many levels. Let me just mention a few:

1. Writing a coherent email would take me much longer than it would to have a conversation. Why would I want to spend this time, for free?

2. I'd have to *describe* my actions and what the software interface shows, or copy/paste screenshots into a Word file. Assuming I manage to write everything I mean, will he really understand all of it exactly?

3. Notice that his first sentence screams one-way communication. "You have feedback? Kindly spend your time composing it, send it our way, and we'll take it under advisement, thank you."

I would have loved to have a conversation, even on the phone. Not just for the richness of information; a conversation engages two people *as people*. It creates a relationship, goodwill, shared history, potential new avenues, and so many other benefits.

Had the designer stayed at the conference that evening, he would have heard the closing keynote speaker, Jared Spool (of experience design fame), describe three Predictors of Success. Here is number two:

"In the last six weeks, have you spent more than two hours watching someone use your design or a competitor's?"

SUPPLEMENTARY RESOURCE: Download "Gil Broza's Process for Effective Feedback Requests" from the book's companion website, **www.TheAgileMindsetBook.info**.

Deferring Decisions

Every August I participate in the City Chase, an "urban adventure" in Toronto. This six-hour-long version of *The Amazing Race* requires a lot of running, walking, even getting wet, and involves some prep work: readying my backpack. This short task has one obvious guideline — keep the backpack light — but other "requirements" are not so clear. I need to know: How hot will it get? Will I need rain gear or a change of clothes? Should I waterproof some items?

Since the answer to "What should I pack?" depends heavily on the weather, I turn to the forecast, which is presumably more accurate the closer it is to Chase day. Here are the forecasts (in Celsius degrees) that led up to the 2012 event:

✦ 14 to 11 days prior: high between 27°C and 29°C, chance of thundershowers

✦ 10 to 8 days prior: high between 24°C and 27°C, sunny

✦ 7 to 4 days prior: high between 23°C and 25°C, isolated showers up to 4mm

✦ 3 to 1 days prior: high of 23°C, cloudy with showers up to 5mm

The actual weather was: high of 22°C, scattered showers, less than 1mm of rain.

As these forecasts are quite inconsistent about both the temperature and the rain, it behooves me to delay packing. I can afford to wait until the morning of the event, when my information about the weather is most current and I know for a fact I'm going. If my mind tends to be foggy in the morning, I might pack the night before. Earlier than that, and I might pack too much, which would slow me down during the Chase.

This is an example of the principle called "defer decisions to the last responsible moment." The tricky part, of course, is knowing *when* that moment is. Making that determination depends heavily on context and experience. In my example, I live in a city where summer weather can be quite fickle and extreme. If the City Chase took place in Phoenix, Arizona, there'd be little doubt about August weather.

When you think about it, *all* work boils down to a long series of decisions and their implementation. Decisions cover who, what, when, where, and how. Some have far-flung implications and some have only localized effect. Some decisions guide the work of entire teams while others affect only you for the next two minutes. You still need to make them, though.

Decision-making relies on information. You hardly ever have complete information, and you never know what you don't know. Having to make a decision now, you might benefit from delaying it some, but how long can you wait? When will the negative consequences of the delay outweigh the benefits of having more information?

Waterfall thinking guides you to collect, vet, and approve all the requirements before you design and implement any solution. Many people believe this allows responsible decision-making, since it's based on maximum information. But in any sizable project, the requirements sign-off milestone occurs *months* before the last responsible moment. Come implementation time, some of those requirements may have changed or become obsolete. The same applies to "big design up front": some of the design might be invalidated, or even proven untenable. Some designs do need to be made early, but not *all* of them.

So, is the best time to make decisions about requirements and design the moment before starting to build? At the micro level, this is correct. I am deciding, this minute, to write in this paragraph that test-driven development (TDD) is a technique for delaying low-level design decisions till the last responsible moment. A few days ago, as I was laying out the ideas for this chapter, I didn't think at this level of detail (and even if I had, I might have decided not to say anything about TDD).

At higher levels of complexity, however, the time to make requirements and design decisions may precede implementation by a while. Agile's use of iterations demonstrates this. The product backlog includes high-level statements of problems and solutions, yet there's no commitment to deliver them; they are merely good ideas the team might get to. As the time to consider an item for implementation draws closer, the cross-functional team understands it better, adds detail, determines acceptance criteria, and explores potential designs (this approach is usually called "gradual refinement"). Nevertheless, they have not decided to actually work on it. That decision arises in iteration planning a few days later, and still, they only make specific *construction* decisions sometime later in the iteration.

When practicing Agile, this principle guides each decision you make. Unfortunately, in every business setting I've encountered, it makes people quite nervous because it bumps against culture and habits that expect decisions to be made early. Making swift decisions confidently often earns you points with others. And if you delay, others might feel that they can't trust you. This principle requires several other principles from the "Individuals and Interactions" department to be present, particularly safety, respect, and trust.

Be aware of the effect of deferring decisions on your *end user*. For instance, consider the work of allocating departure gates for planes at an airport. London's Heathrow Airport does not preallocate gates; passengers wait somewhere in the right terminal, and learn which gate to go to only 10–30 minutes before boarding, as in the following picture:

13:35 Hamburg	BA974	Gate shown 12:45
13:40 Edinburgh	BA1446	Will depart A gates
13:40 Paris CdG	BA314	Gate shown 12:50
13:45 Newcastle	AB5124	Gate shown 12:55
13:50 Shanghai	BA169	Gate shown 12:35
13:50 Athens	BA640	Gate shown 13:00
13:55 San Francisco	AY5527	Gate shown 12:40
14:00 Riyadh	BA263	Gate shown 12:45
14:00 Brussels	BA396	Gate shown 13:10
14:00 Madrid	IB7445	Gate shown 13:10
14:05 Manchester	AB5138	Gate shown 13:33

This approach might work well for the airport operator, but the net effect on this one passenger is a heightened level of stress; every time I fly out of Heathrow, I just can't relax. On the other hand, at my home airport (Toronto Pearson), which like Heathrow moves about 40 million passengers annually but through only two terminals, I know my gate already when I arrive at the airport. I can wait there, and if there's a gate change, I can be sure of hearing about it in a timely manner.

The following are some of the popular heuristics and guidelines for deciding what to work on. Each one has its strengths in certain contexts and not others. Some are described in more detail in the next chapter.

+ "You Aren't Gonna Need It" (YAGNI). To reduce the amount of anticipated work, you could examine each item and ask if you *really* need it. Developers might ask questions like "Do we *really* need to make this package well-rounded and generic?" and "Will we *ever* experience a level of load, scale, or demand to justify this design?" Team members challenge their customers, "As appealing as feature X looks, how *likely* is it to be used enough to justify our investment?" Determining what *not to do* is one of the key sources of high productivity in Agile.

+ "Minimum Viable Product" (MVP). Unless you're 100% certain that the next big initiative is worth undertaking, don't commit to it. Instead, find something smaller but still viable — a subset, perhaps — that will help you decide about the larger initiative.

+ "The simplest thing that could possibly work." When deciding *how* to do something, choose among the various possibilities the simplest solution that delivers the goods. If you don't intend to come back to it after you're done, a throwaway may suffice. Otherwise, produce a simple solution that can evolve into something more complex with little wasted effort. "Simple" does not mean silly, dirty, or barely competent; it means going to the heart of the problem and not adding anything unnecessary.

+ Focus on solving problems you have in the present, then consider addressing future problems. You likely have enough problems today, so deal with them first — just do enough risk analysis to avoid exacerbating tomorrow's problems.

Agile places a premium on customer collaboration and adaptivity, and is leery of certainty. Hence, it offers considerable guidance about deciding what to work on, far beyond the traditionally understood requirements process. From focusing on customer, outcome, and value; through assiduous feedback and learning; and to deferring decisions, the Agile mind-set is keen on making the right difference to the right customer. In the next chapter, we'll see what the mind-set has to say about planning the work for that.

Chapter 3
Planning the Work

As the previous chapter explained, determining what to work on — and what not to work on — is a continual matter in Agile, not reserved only for the beginning. Planning is similar: keeping the valuable end in mind, Agile teams continually determine and validate their next course of action. This chapter explores the Agile approach to planning work.

Effective

Early and frequent delivery of valuable product increments is a top priority in Agile. If you deploy Web or mobile apps and you have millions of users, a week's delay may well mean reduced revenue and lost customers. But what if you're building systems for insurance companies or universities, for example? Should you still deliver early and frequently, even if the business cycle is much longer?

To answer this important question, first consider a bigger question: How do you know that the deliverables are indeed valuable? That they fulfill a need, solve a problem, or achieve users' goals? That they are worth building?

As we saw in the previous chapter, the Agile answer to these questions is to receive timely and actionable feedback from sources that matter. In other words, deciding what to do and delivering it are learning problems. If enough users can give you straight feedback, deploy the product as frequently as possible and sensible, and ask them. Other feedback may come from the product owner, stakeholders, or select early-access users. Either way, if you organize the work and the workers to allow early and frequent feedback, you will reduce (though not eliminate) the odds of being wrong.

Waterfall practitioners also ask for feedback: they test requirements, review designs, and ask users to acceptance-test their deliverables. Agile practitioners do all that too, but differently. The Agile principles give rise to two planning guidelines:

1. Never do *anything* for too long without checking your work.

2. Prefer to get that feedback on *something built*, not only on the idea or specification of it. (Human beings tend to give more useful feedback on something they can use, see, or touch than if they just read about it or reason about an abstraction.)

What this means for planning is that deciding to act on a work item implies getting it to a demonstrable, usable, and preferably deployable state. And if this appears to delay feedback unacceptably, find a smaller subset of the work item that you *can* get to a demonstrable, usable, and preferably deployable state in a timely manner. Work on that one, do the feedback dance, then decide what's next.

Getting the feedback and acting on it takes time and energy from everyone on the team. Sometimes, not everyone is available who should be part of the conversation. And some feedback cycles may well yield a simple "All good, carry on" conclusion. If you're getting the impression that developing a large-ish feature or product element this way is not as fast as doing it the sequential way (requirements — design — construction — testing), you are absolutely right. Agile is deliberately designed this way.

This bears repeating. In the Agile mind-set, being effective is more important than being efficient. If you expect to be wrong some of the time, or if you expect to be right but still make room for unforeseeable opportunities or conditions, then you have to organize for effectiveness: for doing the right thing. Only after you've done that may you consider optimizing the activities involved.

To use language from Lean thinking, the preference is for a good flow of valuable results, and for responsiveness, over keeping workers busy. Of course, workers come at a cost, but bearing the cost might be worthwhile if they are generally spending their time developing the right things. For decades, organizations that develop complex products have been trying to ensure efficiency by keeping workers busy. Their experience has shown that *preferring* efficiency trades off the ability to respond and adapt.

Time-Boxing

Some endeavors in life are "scope-boxed" or "content-boxed": to accomplish the goal, you must finish certain things. To obtain a university degree, for instance, you must complete a set of courses with passing (but not necessarily perfect) grades. To continue eating your meals at home, you must regularly clean the dishes.

Other endeavors are "quality-boxed": to accomplish the goal, you must reach a higher standard than simply getting the nominal job done. If you only sort-of follow a pastry recipe, you're not likely to produce an edible or attractive pastry. If you put together only 990 pieces of a 1,000-piece jigsaw puzzle, you probably won't hang that odd-looking picture on your wall.

Yet other endeavors are "time-boxed": you only have a certain window of time to deal with them. It doesn't matter how much or how well you pack for an overseas trip if you miss your plane. You only have an hour or two to finish a proctored school exam. Children spend a certain number of hours in the classroom every week whether they finish their studies or not.

Every undertaking has a primary constraint. It may also have secondary constraints, but to accomplish the purpose, you need to arrange the work and the workers in response to the primary constraint. Constraints drive process and behavior, and thereby results.

In the '90s, Agile thinking arose out of business and user frustration with large software development efforts. It turned out that in many cases, users preferred receiving *something* working early to receiving *everything* maybe-working late. Even though most development projects had explicit constraints on time, scope, quality, and cost, those constraints did not drive behavior and results effectively. The deadline was months away, the scope large, and quality left to the end. The early Agilists discovered that imposing *deliberate* constraints on the team could yield great results. Agile is big on doing precisely that, and its favorite constraint on value-producing work is time.

The primary Agile mechanism for putting time constraints on large work is the iteration (which the Scrum framework calls "sprint"). The idea is that before the team starts working, they determine the time-box: *when* they will stop working, for instance in exactly 14 days. The oft-missed element that makes the iteration boundary useful — rather than a nuisance and an interruption to flow — is what the team plans for that time-box. Instead of just intending to be busy or make best effort during this time, they collaboratively determine the *outcomes* of the iteration. To practitioners of Agile time-boxing, it doesn't matter whether they have one hour, one day, or one week to make progress (at a sustainable pace); they simply identify the best results they'll have accomplished at the end.

Since iterations are intentionally short, iteration plans (in Scrum, "sprint backlogs") include only a handful of valuable outcomes. These typically include product features and capabilities. Some outcomes explicitly reduce risk — generally, that of shipping the wrong thing or shipping late. And some outcomes, or even entire iterations, may be time-boxed experiments: they start with a hypothesis and end in learning. In other words, the iteration has the potential to be highly informative; what information would be most useful right now? A hypothesis may be about the product, the user, the implementation, or anything else related to the work objectives. An Agile team would create a shippable increment to yield the most learning and feedback necessary to prove or disprove their hypothesis.

The product owner is usually in the best place to identify the next most important outcomes. Nevertheless, the Agile preference is to make that determination collaboratively, and in consensus, with the delivery team and the team lead. If the team believes that they can indeed produce those outcomes, they make a plan that they can commit to, so their customers and stakeholders can proceed with their own planning.

An Agile iteration makes sense only if three conditions apply:

1. The team must have a good idea about the top few valuable outcomes, so they know what to include in their plan. (Teams that deal exclusively with production support can usually see only a few days ahead, so they can't plan iterations well.)

2. The iteration needs to be long enough for the team to accomplish meaningful results. It also needs to be short enough for the outcomes to remain valuable and for the team to "see the end" and maintain a sense of urgency.

3. The iteration must be disturbance-free. A team can't finish its planned work if it can't focus or it has many other obligations.

When a new demand materializes, the team must be able to say, "Let's consider this at the next iteration planning meeting" (unless the urgency of the demand trumps the importance of their commitment).

Many software development teams discover that their sweet spot for fulfilling these conditions is to have a two-week-long iteration. Smaller teams working on rapid-turnaround technologies and platforms even opt for one-week iterations. While commonly used, there is no magic about these numbers, and some teams find three- or four-week-long iterations more useful in their context (unless their reason for choosing longer cycles is to accommodate mini-Waterfalls in them).

Teams favor keeping all their iterations the same length, since a regular cadence, or rhythm, helps them establish routine and frees their minds to deal with bigger concerns. However, as long as the three conditions apply, a team may occasionally plan for a different-length iteration, for instance around holidays or short deadlines.

At the start of each time-box (typically an iteration, but possibly also an entire product release), a team would choose top-priority outcomes to fit into their time-box. When the time-box ends, they have ideally finished working on those items. In Kanban,[1] another approach to work that often draws interest from Agile practitioners, teams also work on the outcomes in rough priority sequence, but replace the time-box with another artificial constraint: they limit the number of items they take on at once. In this mode — known as "flow" — they complete a new item every few hours or days. Some Agile teams superimpose flow on iterations: throughout their time-boxes, they only have a small number of items in flight. You might be wondering, then, isn't flow simpler or good enough? What's the use of iterations if you can have flow?

Planning with a short horizon puts pressure on the planners to choose what really matters. The regular "heartbeat" of iterations creates scheduled opportunities for business, management, and team members to review those choices, see progress, seek feedback, and respond to changes. Agile welcomes change, but not willy-nilly and not any old time; the best time to change plan contents is at the iteration boundary. Therefore, it's also a synchronization opportunity if several teams are involved. During the iteration, the team focuses on what they recently believed to be most important, and they can expect the contents to change little. Having "pinned down" their work, they can make promises or forecasts about what would be ready when the iteration is over. And when the iteration ends, they can step back, relax and reflect, and prepare for a new cycle. Iterations are akin to punctuation in long text.

> "We tried planning scope-boxed iterations. We'd pick a goal, estimate the needed time, and keep working through the iteration until we had achieved the goal. We found the temptation to 'just add one more thing' or 'just fix one more bug' meant the delivery kept slipping and slipping. Our customers were kept waiting too long for their updates and fixes.
>
> "Then we tried time-boxing iterations to four weeks. Our internal customers got impatient and wanted to throw 'just one more thing' in, else they'd have to wait another month. Next we tried one-week iterations, but their increments weren't enough for the team to get any feeling of progress.
>
> "We've settled on two-week iterations. That duration allows us to pick a meaningful goal that feels like an actual achievement, but it's short enough that people are willing to wait for the next iteration."
>
> – *Ian Brockbank, Agile Team Leader at Cirrus Logic, Edinburgh*

With work progressing in short iterations, the consequence of being wrong is much lower. The visibility over months of development is much higher, enabling trust and collaboration. Product owners get their important concerns addressed; delivery teams get regular reinforcement that their effort is worthwhile. Both roles discover quickly whether they over-ask, over-commit, or over-build. While iterations are not the only mechanism to establish these feedback loops, they facilitate them and make them a matter of routine.

Managing Complexity

A team was building GPS-based navigation software to put on large-screen cellphones. This was in 2004, when such phones were new, slow, and unable to download map data from the Internet. They decided to write a "compiler" to translate relational map data into a compressed binary form to store on the phone. So they formed two teams: the application team and the compiler team.

Modeling the phone application on an existing navigation device, the compiler team felt the requirements were obvious, so it produced a compact, generic design for the compiler. As development progressed, it turned out to be too complex and difficult to use, and many requirements turned out to be unnecessary and incorrect.

The compiler team, together with the product owner (who happened to manage Engineering), chose to rewrite its main component. The design was easier to use this time...but the resulting database didn't match up with the navigation needs.

It took an eleventh-hour effort of refactoring and rewriting compiler code in lockstep with the navigation application to get it right.

The team in this story put 12 person-months into writing the compiler before realizing they had missed the mark. With this magnitude of sunk costs, what should they do: Look for minimal alterations to its ill-fitting design, or redo it?

It's not unusual for software teams to find themselves in this position. In many organizations, a situation like this triggers blame, retrenchment, justification, and overtime. The textbook responses — "collect better requirements next time," "get the architecture right first," "have our star developers work on critical pieces" — just don't seem to work reliably. These problems plague the competent, the intelligent, and the experienced. According to the Agile mind-set, the reason is simple: up-front planning is not the best approach to managing complexity.

A better, safer approach to managing complexity is evolution, also called emergence. Rather like evolution in nature (only much faster), a solution grows in response to needs. Throughout its growth, it adapts to new learning about the needs and the implementation, as well as to changes in them. The solution evolves to address the needs *and no more*. Its design must be pliable and simple enough so future adaptations are practical and require little correction or undoing. Agile planning takes all this into consideration, but it's not easy; it requires distinguishing the parts that are likely to change from those that are not. Collaboration and consensus in planning should mitigate both difficulty and risk.

If the team in the story had been able to go back in time, what could they have done differently? Rather than split off into two functional subteams, they could have stayed together, implementing each new navigation feature in both the application and the map compiler. They might have started by implementing the simplest case: the map has a single street, and you navigate from one end of it to the other. (Agile practitioners call this tactic "Start with one.") Then, include two streets in the map, and navigate from one to the other with a single turn. Add more streets and more turns, including time-limited ones. Continue building combinations and exceptions. Behaviors of application, database, and compiler would thus grow in lockstep.

Over time, the growth in system complexity (due to adding capabilities) increases the cost of change. Along the way, the cost grows even more due to the buildup of *cruft*: leftovers, stuff "we might use someday," shoddy construction, and mismatches between design intent and actual use. The higher the cost, the longer it takes to achieve desired results. While change is never free of charge, the Agile mind-set guides practitioners to keep it low by planning and building for changeability. And if some desired change is hard to make, they must adapt the design first; otherwise, their band-aid solution would cause a much larger increase in the cost of *later* change.

Backlog

Even Agile teams that don't use Scrum rely on one of its central planning artifacts: the product backlog. It is a simple and straightforward mechanism, though it is often misunderstood.

Traditional methods call for maintaining the list of requirements separately from the designs that satisfy them and also separately from the tasks that implement the designs. The Agile backlog has largely eliminated this separation. Since Agile teams progress by addressing a few needs and outcomes at a time, as opposed to implementing a comprehensive solution in one go, they consider each need or outcome a backlog item. As they reflect on each item, they enrich it with their thoughts about its design, dependencies, technical details, implementation tasks, and the like.

The chosen term for this artifact, "backlog," is quite clever. Instead of staring up a disheartening mountain of work, we can believe that it's all downhill and we're almost there — we only have these items left. There may still be a lot of work, but the emphasis is on finishing, not starting.

The focal point of each backlog item is always its value. If you read a backlog, its items spell out what the product can help accomplish, as opposed to how it's built. As such, items are end-to-end: they indicate how someone or something engages with the system from one end to produce a valued result at another end. A common tool for capturing backlog items is the "story." Told from the perspective of the person or thing that engages with the product, the story describes either the problem the team is solving or the intended solution.

Some teams make a list of such items, and then spend a while producing a design and task list to cover all of the items. These teams assume that every item is required, so they have effectively given up an Agile value: adaptation. In their view, the backlog is a project plan. But if you have the Agile mind-set and adaptation is important to you, the backlog becomes something else: *a list of things that the team might get to*. The backlog is a transparent means of planning work. If the team doesn't get to some of them, that's not due to laziness or incompetence: it's because they have learned of better things to do.

Treating backlog items as possible, rather than mandatory, means you keep your options open. Altering scope, by changing items that the team hasn't started yet, can thus be both low-cost and low-ceremony. Scope flexibility is critical if you place a higher premium on other project parameters, such as schedule and cost. However, you must prioritize the items, and keep revisiting their priorities.

This approach is radically different from designing and implementing to satisfy a complete set of requirements. You need an empowered person or group to determine priorities; that is typically the "product owner," the voice of the business — not the team's manager. Many people need to weigh in on priorities, because context changes quickly. Working on items from "later" — even just doing prep work — is discouraged, because the work may turn out to be wasted, and the top of the backlog is more important. Agile practitioners don't build the future now, but, contrary to popular impression, they *do* take likely futures into consideration and strive not to compromise them in the interest of the here and now.

Planning for Less

The previous chapter mentioned the "You Aren't Gonna Need It" (YAGNI) heuristic. Agile teams that practice YAGNI welcome discussions about potential features, aspects, and quality requirements, yet feel free to push back on some. They truly believe that doing so is in their customers' best interest. After all, when the

YAGNIs are stripped away from proposed work, plenty of important work probably remains. If the team can expect to iterate more on their product — if it's not an "ask for it now or wait another year to get it" situation — they are effectively minimizing scope so they can quickly turn a valuable product increment around. As the popular saying goes, they "travel light."

> The YAGNI heuristic also has many uses in personal planning. Examples of where applying it would have helped me or my family, in hindsight, include:
>
> ✦ Packing a bigger bag than necessary for a trip
>
> ✦ Buying a large digital picture frame
>
> ✦ Preparing too many dishes for a dinner party
>
> ✦ Getting a second item at 50% off when we only needed one

This logical approach works well in some organizations, but in many others, emotions sabotage it. When you want something done, or you invest the time thinking about some feature or enhancement, don't you get a little attached to it? Isn't hearing "forget it, you won't *need* that" really a bit disheartening? And what if you've already promised, or even suggested it, to a customer or a manager?

Despite personal conviction, we can never predict with 100% accuracy that something will not be needed or worth building. Instead of a strict "You Aren't Gonna Need It" approach, which amounts to in-scope/out-of-scope, teams are able to collaborate better with their customers and stakeholders through simple prioritization: You Don't Need It *Now*. When someone approaches them with a non-urgent bright idea, a request from management, or sensible user feedback, they say, "Let's stick to our current iteration plan, and consider the new thing's priority for a later iteration." The item ends up someplace on the backlog, and the whole exchange has been less judgmental and more respectful.

With this approach, which is more inclusive than minimalist YAGNI, backlogs may grow rather large. However, as long as items are inserted according to their consensus-based priority, the team is able to keep their options open and their working relationship positive. Typically, one of two things happens: the backlog's low-priority tail grows longer but never actually gets implemented (because it's not worth implementing), or its higher-priority side grows denser as both team and customer learn more about their product. This isn't the much-maligned phenomenon of "scope creep"; instead, it's keeping plans current with reality and needs. Since that backlog will be consumed one iteration at a time, you will have many opportunities to change your mind.

Commitments

Many clients ask me a variation of this question: "How can we balance long-term planning and commitment with flexibility?" This question isn't so much about the length of the backlog, but about how much of it they will commit to, and at what level of detail.

Nothing in Agile says you can't plan far into the future. Such planning tends to limit the potential for change and responsiveness, which is fine in some contexts. However, if you do want to respond to change of mind, understanding, or circumstance, long-term planning is wasteful and creates false expectations.

To answer the question, you must first understand the purpose of planning *in your context*. Is it to know and control costs? To make promises? To support planning of other initiatives? To comply with regulation? Each purpose has its place, and it emphasizes certain aspects of planning. Is that value greater than the cost of planning and later changing the plans?

I began both this book and my previous one, *The Human Side of Agile*, the same way: I did a chartering exercise to understand what they were about. Planning the content was different, though. When I started the first book, I could identify maybe half the scope; the content and layout morphed continuously, so a detailed plan for writing didn't make sense. For this book, it was easier to make a list of in-scope topics and identify the high-level points to make. In fact, planning the layout — organizing the material into chapters and sections — reinforced my conviction in the content itself. This organization changed very little throughout the writing, even with feedback.

Agile planning must strike a fine balance between determining the future and keeping options open. When teams do have to make promises that reach weeks and months into the future, the "defer decisions," "effective," and "outcome" principles kick in. These guide the team and the product owner to discuss which problems they'll solve and for what customer value. They ensure that the team is committing to the right thing and can accomplish it in a timely manner once they begin working on it. This early analysis yields decisions that must be made early and defers those that can be made later, just in time.

For undertakings that take several people several months, a "nested cycles" planning pattern seems to be useful. Initially, people discuss problems, capabilities, and solutions at a high level. They plan product *releases* that align with business cadence and cover some of these high-level items; a good time frame for a release tends to be six to 12 weeks (not too short, not too long). They plan the first release with more rigor than the later ones, which are too nebulous to justify reliable promises. Inside the release, they plan the more fine-grained cycle — the one-, two-, or three-week-long iteration — by refining and decomposing solutions.

In some traditional methods, the people who plan the work breakdown and schedule are different from those who do the work. The planners — usually managers, project managers, and team leads — may have more information and planning experience than the doers. By specializing in planning, they free up "doer" time for the doing.

In the Agile mind-set, this seemingly efficient division of labor doesn't always yield good plans. Instead, the preference is to have the doers (the delivery team) take on certain planning activities, because they have the most pertinent, current, and detailed information. They identify implementation details, tasks, dependencies, and estimates. Since the information comes from them, and they have to live with the consequences, they are more likely to own and want to carry out the execution plan.

> This effect was palpable at a recent iteration retrospective. At my suggestion, the project's leadership had — for the first time — asked the delivery team to estimate their work, instead of relying exclusively on the development manager and the team leads to do that. During the retrospective, the team highlighted their involvement in estimation as a positive. When I asked, "What was particularly good about that?" the impassioned response was, "Because we know the work and how long the tasks take!"

Since the doers are assumed to form a tight team, they can do such planning in facilitated activities that draw out their shared wisdom and reduce personal bias. When they make a commitment, it's a *team commitment* to be done with the whole work. It is not a collection of individual commitments, with each person promising to work on tasks that are obviously theirs. In their planning meetings, indeed at all times, individuals will avoid making any statement that might commit a team to something the team hasn't examined for themselves.

A company in the information search business was replacing its Web portal. The product team (VP Marketing plus two analysts) had a very clear picture of the new site in mind: before bringing Agile in, they had spent months writing its specification. Senior management expected development to take four months. Before committing to anything, the team spent two hours informally estimating the spec (which had been recast as stories). Their analysis: 11 months. So, instead of launching into a "best-effort" development rush, their next step was to reset management's expectations and trim the scope.

Splitting Items

Inevitably, some work items will be large. Valuable as they are, what if spending the time to fully implement them delays feedback, reduces revenue potential, or affects some other important outcome?

This tension is normal, and every team experiences it regularly. Not all responses to it are helpful, though. The most common unhelpful ones are:

+ Extend the iteration so the items fit.

+ Chip away at the items until done, whether the work crosses iteration boundaries or not.

+ Tell the team to cram more work into the iteration ("increase velocity").

+ Break the work down into small tasks and assign them to the team's experts for maximum efficiency and utilization.

Because these approaches contradict the Agile values, beliefs, and principles, applying them results in zero Agile benefit. If implementation happens to be a slam dunk and there's no value in showing or deploying interim results, these approaches might get the job done, even though they won't make anyone happy (especially the third item).

The Agile response to big work is to split (or decompose) it into small work. The key, *which is often missed*, is that each small work item should make a difference and fit within the planning time-box (the iteration). Each smaller item results in one or more of the following outcomes:

+ Delivering value

+ Learning something important

+ Removing a problem, doubt, or risk

You might notice this is the exact profile of those valuable outcomes that typically populate the backlog. They are end-to-end, useful, "vertical slices" of the bigger item. They are neither tasks for the delivery team nor determined based on team members' specialties. The product owner and/or the delivery team simply identify a mode of splitting that seems to best fit their context and needs. If some of the resulting pieces are still too large, they repeat the exercise. The following popular questions help to decompose items:

+ "What's our biggest unknown here?"

+ "What's the best thing we could learn about this?"

+ "Which 20% of this item would yield 80% of the return?" (*the Pareto principle*)

+ "If we could spend only X units of time or money on this, what would we choose to do?" (*this is the self-imposed constraint tactic*)

+ "Which assumption or hypothesis should we prove or disprove?" (*this question comes from Lean Startup*)

+ "Which part has the highest cost of delay?" (*this is a key question in Lean thinking*)

Splitting is useful for more reasons than supporting small timeboxes. Product owners frequently hear that the price tag for certain items exceeds what they're willing to pay. In these cases, they can figure out how much it's worth to them and ask, "What can I have for that cost?" What commonly follows is a splitting activity, in which some of the least-important pieces are simply discarded. In general, splitting shortens the time to learning and feedback; it's a way to follow the guideline "Never do *anything* for too long without checking your work."

Once the team has identified a sequence of these smaller items — sometimes even just the start of such a sequence — finishing the big work is no longer an all-or-nothing proposition. In the first iteration, they might finish a couple of small pieces, seek feedback and apply learning, then continue. Even though the whole thing is not ready yet, the rest is in the backlog. This approach typically results in less rushing, fewer loose ends to tie up, and finer-grain control of the work.

The development of a messaging application reached the feature of group messaging. The full capability required a number of teams working over a couple of weeks. This is one sequence of substories they considered:

1. Start simple: send a single message to a predefined user group whose members are all online.

2. Same as #1, but one of the recipients is offline. (The thrust of both stories would be feedback on usability — a high risk for their product.)

3. Facilitate integration testing for this feature in production-like environments. (A constant challenge for this team.)

4. Ensure stability and reliability when multiple groups are sending messages at the same time. (Expected to be a high risk once the feature goes public.)

All substories having to do with managing groups would be done later: their feedback-worthiness and risk were lower than that of every other substory.

Just as the team aspires to get each item to a demonstrable, usable, and preferably deployable state, so it should do with the smaller pieces. Having laid out their sequence, however, team members (and their managers) sometimes get nervous at this point. Since each small piece often requires work on several parts of the product — in software, these would be user interface, behavioral logic, and foundation — and those parts require different skills and time investment, working item by item seems inefficient. And in many cases, that is absolutely true. This approach is not meant to make work efficient but effective, and to *reduce the cost of later changes* by making the following possible:

✦ Everyone has time to change their minds about elements of the big work that haven't been started yet.

✦ If the team runs late, postponing lowest-priority elements to a later time doesn't incur overhead.

✦ The team manages many risks up front. By truly completing pieces along the way, they neither squeeze testing into the very end, nor get surprised by nasty defects when they have little time left.

✦ If more important business results require attention, the team can switch to working on them, with few items left hanging.

Even though Agile does not ascribe the same importance to efficiency as it does to effectiveness, feedback, and embracing change, many Agile projects do turn out to be also faster and cheaper than their Waterfall counterparts. This doesn't happen due to optimizing at the team member and task level. It happens because the team works on fewer items, and what it does start it finishes quickly. Also, many teams have discovered that the self-imposed constraint of making work small enough for the time-box forces them to produce simpler designs, incur less waste, and experience fewer nasty surprises.

Estimating

People rely on estimates in many walks of life, even when they are clearly inaccurate. For example, pregnant women receive due-date predictions from their doctors; although fewer than one in 20 give natural birth on their due date, that information helps them plan for the occasion.

Various forms of the practice of estimation appear in most Agile implementations. By knowing the cost of work items, we can decide when to fit them in and whether to look for alternatives. That said, useful estimation of work in business settings has a spotty track record: too often, estimates are unreliable and give rise to dysfunctional behavior. Most people consider estimation a necessary evil and approach it with reluctance. They pad their real estimates, because being wrong carries unpleasant personal consequences. Often, others discredit or modify their numbers. And even when presented with **DISCLAIMERS AND CAVEATS IN BIG BOLD TEXT**, estimates have an exasperating habit of turning into commitments. How else to explain the made-up word "guesstimate"?

A few years ago I designed an estimation exercise for my Agile courses. Using a projector, I show pictures of parking lots in Toronto and ask the students to estimate the number of legal spaces, whether occupied or not. Some cars are already parked in those lots, and solid lines demarcate the spaces. Each picture is shot at street level, not from above. All the students are adults who have driven and parked various cars in North America for years. In other words, they are all subject matter experts.

At 32 parking spaces, the first lot is the smallest, and I even show it from both ends. Everybody writes down their estimate in silence, to prevent even accidentally biasing one another. When everyone has a number, I tabulate them in a spreadsheet on the screen. I also show the average, but keep the correct answer to myself. We repeat the process with the second lot, which has 56 spaces.

At this point, everybody is excited to learn the real numbers...and shocked to discover how off their estimates were! The range of estimates is quite wide, so we look at the group's average. In every one of the last 11 groups that did this exercise — 183 people in total — the averages were quite a bit lower than the real numbers. The averages ranged from 58% to 82% for the first lot, and from 52% to 82% for the second lot.

However, we always observe an interesting phenomenon. In each class, the ratio between the second lot's average estimate and the first lot's average estimate hovers between 1.26 and 2. The average of these ratios across all 11 groups was 1.57. This is almost identical to the real ratio, which is 1.75.

All I asked people to do was to estimate parking spaces. They mostly got the numbers wrong, both individually and as a group. But if we produce a naive group estimate — the average of individual ones — we discover that they are pretty good at relative estimation. On the whole, these groups have decided that the second lot is about 57% larger than the first one (remember, the true number is 75%). Agilists have long claimed that people are better at rough relative sizing than at absolute sizing of work. Hence the practice of estimating stories with points, which are relative by nature, instead of with person-days.

Having discussed this, we repeat the estimation and tabulation exercise with a third lot. Its picture is a poorly pasted together panorama of the parking lot of my kids' school, and a huge tree obstructs much of the middle. This time, group averages range between 61% and 116% of the real number (175), and the average of these group estimates is 85% of the real number.

The groups succeed better with the third lot than the second lot, because they receive feedback on their estimates. It's the best feedback they could wish for: the real numbers, which they use to calibrate their estimates. Interestingly, in each group the spread of individual estimates remains large, with folks estimating even three times under or over. But taking the average of each group, the estimate bears closer resemblance to reality. Agile teams give themselves similar feedback during reviews and retrospectives when they compare their plans to actual deliverables.

After I reveal the right answer and we examine the averages and ratios, we move on to the fourth and last parking lot. It is in the center of a squarish strip mall, so large I also show a sweeping video panorama. By this time, the groups have had enough feedback on individual and shared estimates, and their results are better. Group estimates range between 77% and 122% of the real number, and the average group estimate clocks in at 94%. Each *group* is doing better now, even though *individuals* are still way off; in fact, only a handful of people ever estimated two or more lots within 10% of the correct numbers.

One explanation of the improvement is practice accompanied by feedback and awareness. But that's only part of the story. At play here is the phenomenon known as the Wisdom of Crowds,[2] which predicts that a group may be wiser than its individuals under certain conditions. My estimation activity meets all three conditions: all participants have basic knowledge of the subject matter, they offer their input individually without biasing each other, and there's a meaningful way to compute a group answer. Many Agile teams use the Planning Poker estimation activity, which is also designed to fulfill these conditions.

When it comes to team estimation, the team doesn't have to be large for the Wisdom of Crowds phenomenon to kick in. Agile teams capitalize on this fact and prefer to estimate together, rather than have a single person (such as a technical lead) produce estimates. The single person may appear to possess the most knowledge and might take the least time to produce an estimate, but *using* his or her estimate may be a risky proposition — it came out of a single human brain.

Correctly estimating the size of a parking lot from its picture ought to be *easy*, but the 183 intelligent adults in my courses did poorly. Imagine estimating work that involves dependencies, uncertainties, and special expertise. Moreover, in knowledge work, people rarely perform the exact same task twice, so most everything they estimate is effectively new. How well would they estimate such tasks?

These are all objective challenges, which presumably can be managed away by investing enough time to learn about the work. But there are subjective challenges too. People are hopeless optimists; we like to assume that work ought to proceed with no serious hiccup (life would be rather miserable if we didn't do that). Even when we admit some risks are likely, we struggle mightily to account for them; our many cognitive biases certainly don't help.

What about estimating simple repetitive tasks that each team member can perform?

In 2012 my family moved to a house one street over. In preparation, we invited five different movers to estimate the work. Their representatives paraded through our house with clipboards; only a couple appeared physically strong enough to have ever moved furniture.

Unlike product development, a house move should be easy to estimate. It's only manual labor, and the few tasks involved are predictable and repetitive: disassemble (partially), load, carry, unload, assemble, and so on. The work is additive and requires little specialization. Large items might require two people, but collaboration among more movers makes little difference. The drive to our new house was negligible and nobody had to wait for elevators. Estimating this work in person-hours actually makes sense. In our minds, we compared it to our neighbors' recent move out of a similarly appointed house.

The lowest estimate was 18 person-hours ("but no more than 27"). Another was 24. The movers my wife had used at work came in at 36 hours; as this was "obviously, outrageously" high, we threw out their estimate. On a recommendation, we hired other movers whose phone estimate was for 27 hours. In each case, we would pay by the hour.

Do you ever participate in a mid-iteration review, or use a burndown chart, to assess the likelihood of finishing on time? We did that four hours into the move, and it was depressing. The actual move spanned two days and took 40 person-hours, during which the movers barely took breaks.

Guidelines for Agile Estimation

If you believe that estimation can be useful in your situation and that you can respond helpfully to wrong estimates, the Agile mind-set includes guidance to mitigate some of your estimation risks.

Small and medium. First, don't bother estimating the very small or very large because your error will be high. Split large items or aggregate small ones into more manageable pieces. Knowledge workers seem to estimate more correctly when the work falls in the range of a few days to a couple of weeks. Relative sizing is particularly powerful on this scale. By splitting larger items before estimating them, and regularly estimating only small- and medium-size work, a team gets a lot more practice with estimation, and increases their sample size to a point where averages start making statistical sense.

Big picture. Similarly, don't try to produce a precise estimate by dissecting an item into many tiny ones and then summing up their estimates. You're likely to miss some tasks, which will invalidate your total numbers. Instead, seek to understand the item's main pieces and risks, and go with gut feel. Use only a small set of possible estimates to avoid the lure of impossible precision.

Team-based estimation. The team owns the work, so the team owns the estimate. That means they produce it collaboratively. Start by making sure that everyone understands the work the same way, especially what it means to be done with it. Ensure that people don't bias each other (otherwise, the estimate isn't really collaborative: it's mostly a function of the first number mentioned). Rely on the Wisdom of Crowds phenomenon to smooth out individuals' inevitable mistakes and cognitive biases.

Team-based units. Since the team owns the work, use team units. Story points are an example of team units, whereas "person-days" relate to some hypothetical average team member and preclude collaboration. Team units imply the whole team taking ownership of a deliverable, and implicitly account for members helping each other out. Moreover, the use of such units dissuades the team from breaking down stories to a series of functional steps (such as analysis, writing tests, coding, running tests), which perpetuates individual specialties and reduces teamwork.

Outcome vs. busyness. Teams sometimes get hung up on detailed planning with precise hourly task estimates, which makes it hard to see the forest for the trees (and suggests false accuracy and confidence). Instead, rely on the "results" and "outcome" principles: focus on the iteration goal and commitment, and on the team's results, rather than on maximizing individual inputs. What value will the team deliver? How will they make a difference? With enough repetition of actual value delivery, the team will develop a good sense for sizing work and for how much it can fit in a cycle.

If it doesn't work, change it. A common practice of choosing an iteration's stories is to know the team's velocity (the number of work units they can accomplish in an iteration), estimate each candidate story in those units, and choose a set of stories whose numbers add up close to that velocity. But some teams just don't seem to produce reliable estimates to make their velocity calculations useful. In such cases, other Agile-friendly options are available. For instance, use the one-question process of asking "Do we think these candidates would fit in the iteration?" and having all team members respond at the same time (to avoid bias). Unless the answer is a resounding yes, modify the set until it is a yes.

Ideal vs. actual. Lastly, distinguish the ideal estimate — how long the work would take with no interruption or disaster — from its actual, calendar duration. Estimation is hard enough when you consider all the other claims on workers' time, such as meetings and responding to unplanned work. Invoking the "simplicity" principle, you might focus on how long the work *should take* under ideal conditions and, separately from that, get data for the typical ratio between ideal and actual.

In my area of expertise — software development — the ratio of ideal time to actual time is downright appalling. A lot of people get in trouble because they won't admit, to their managers or to themselves, how much time is legitimately spent on non-value-adding work.

Done!

An Agile team strives to move their work items to *done*, regardless of how they represent those items (stories, tickets, use cases, or other artifacts). Every team establishes and later refines a definition of "Done" (DoD) according to their context. While "Done" differs from team to team, it always has the same premise: we no longer need to touch this item, and can move on to something else.

In a functional, sequential development life cycle, each function also defines "Done." For business analysts, it is "the requirements are ready for hand-off/approval." For programmers, it tends to be "works on my machine." In the Agile view, these isolated activities don't deliver value, only entire work items do. Therefore, an item is "Done" after closing the loop with its requester so no one has to do any more work. In most software development teams, done-ness includes multiple conditions such as "coded," "reviewed," "build updated," "tests updated," "tested," "accepted," "defects fixed," and many more.

The primary purpose of an Agile team is to deliver value steadily. Since developing a valuable product takes many skills and abilities, the team is cross-functional. In naive Agile software development implementations, that covers only programmers and testers. This combination of specialists typically limits the scope of their definition of "Done." Successful implementations tend to be more inclusive of skill and function, and their definition of "Done" covers more of the work involved in defining and delivering work items.

The scope of the DoD correlates to the team's makeup. Therefore, anything the team leaves out of the definition of "Done" has to be managed separately. For example, in one company the database team belonged to a different organization, and used a different process than the programmer-and-tester teams. The latter couldn't include the software's performance expectations in their "Done" because the former controlled database optimizations. In another example, a company managed technical publications separately from development, so Agile teams could not include "user documentation ready" in their "Done." Such separate management (which tends to correspond to the organizational hierarchy) usually results in delays, bottlenecks, and rework.

For an increment to be "Done," all the pieces have to be there. If a team contemplates some business logic, they should consider the tests for it as well. If they plan a user-facing feature that depends on structural modifications to the database, they had better also develop the code to apply those modifications. In each example, the different pieces now go together, and the team can genuinely say that the feature may be rolled out. It is a true increment, not just the part visible to the user. Some organizations don't have the ability to produce true increments yet, so they rely on a concentrated "hardening" effort to make several "Done" items release-worthy.

As time goes by, more and more increments accumulate in the "Done" column. Several popular patterns describe what to do with those items:

1. Release after several consecutive iterations (this is the nested cycles patterns described earlier).

2. Release every iteration.

3. Release each item as it becomes ready (this is known as Continuous Delivery; the overall process might use timeboxes or flow).

Patterns 1 and 2 are quite common. Choosing between them has a lot to do with organizational context, business cadence, maturity, and technical discipline. When a large organization adopts Agile, starting with pattern 1 is often hard enough though valuable. Graduating to pattern 2 takes another shift in team structure, development and testing approaches, communications, and management. Pattern 3 takes these investments to new levels altogether.

Remember that iterations are a self-imposed constraint that facilitates feedback, learning, and change. Splitting work items, whether across or inside iterations, achieves similar purposes. However, Agile does not oblige you to deploy any item once it's finished. In other words, developing product increments, which is a technical matter, can remain separate from releasing them to the customer or the market, which is a business matter. Agile's "cadence" principle only encourages practitioners to release working product regularly, and to do so at a frequency that best supports the business's rhythm.

Releasing a product increment always carries some level of overhead: testing, packaging, documenting, responding to users of the new increment, and so forth. Smart organizations work on deployability from day one and continue to keep release costs and barriers low. The more frequently you'll want to release product, the lower you'll need to keep the cost of doing so.

If you don't have the Agile mind-set yet, observing a team's planning session might make you scratch your head. Why are so many people getting together just to plan for a couple of weeks? Don't they care for efficiency? Why do they keep asking to simplify, split, remove, or defer work items? Why do they avoid making large commitments?

It's not easy to deduce the Agile values and principles merely from watching common planning practices, which explains the bad reputation Agile has received in certain circles where other mind-sets rule. That is also why you should be careful, if you're interested in Agile, about starting your journey by adopting only sprints and stories. It's the thinking behind them that makes the difference: being effective and collaborative, committing only to the committable, evolving complexity rather than planning for it, and time-boxing as a deliberate constraint.

Now that you have looked at making decisions in the previous chapter, and at planning the work in this chapter, the next obvious step is to examine *doing* the work. Before we can do that, though, we'll consider a bigger matter: the people who do the work. That is the subject of the next two chapters.

SUPPLEMENTARY RESOURCE: Download "Planning with the Agile Mind-Set" checklist from the book's companion website, **www.TheAgileMindsetBook.info**.

Chapter 4
Engaging People

In February 2001, 17 people composed the Agile Manifesto. Of everything they could have written and did write, they deliberately decided to start by saying that while there was value in processes and tools, they valued "individuals and interactions" more.

The Manifesto's authors had made their names and careers in software development, the profession sometimes associated with brainy loners in dark rooms, eating pizza in front of glaring screens. Yet, they had agreed that the people who do the work, and how they interact, matter more than how they do the work.*

---

* In complex adaptive systems, such as software development organizations, the interactions are even more critical than the people.

Some of the better-known Agile practices and attitudes were dis-covered decades ago. In the mid-'90s, the entire package — the Agile *mind-set* — started taking form. I am writing this book in 2014–15; to this day, putting people before process remains the most ignored, misunderstood, and elusive element of the mind-set. This chapter explores how Agile sees the individual; the next chapter dives into the interactions of those individuals when they work in teams.

People Are Not Resources

It wasn't until I got into development management in 2001 that I started hearing the word "resource" in reference to people. I'd hear statements like:

"We have five resources on that project."

"The offshore contractor is assigning four testing resources."

"We're hiring two more senior development resources this quarter."

Many people don't think twice about this wording, which reflects the now-discredited "Theory X" of worker motivation[1] and puts process ahead of people. Considering people as countable, fungible, divisible resources is everywhere. People even do it to themselves; at one standup meeting I observed, a developer said to the Scrum-Master, "I'm a free resource now, what should I do next?"

A resource can be measured, divided, moved, exploited, and traded. *You are a person.* Would you like to be measured, divided, moved, exploited, or traded?

Many organizational cultures still view staff as an expense instead of an investment. Even in the highly creative, insanely complex, and never-repeating activity of software development (in other words, the antithesis of the factory), management attempts to maximize staff uti-lization, usually by multiplexing people across concurrent activities.

Calling people "resources" objectifies them. It implies having or needing a certain control over them. It ignores the social frameworks that people create, for better or worse. It reflects the Theory X belief that you need to extract labor out of them, since they won't work willingly. You are a person. Can others really control you? Are you truly motivated by nothing other than money, title, perks, or power? The word "resource" isn't without merit, it's simply misguided. The real resource is people's willingness to dedicate their energy on their employer's behalf.[2]

Consider an example. Let's say another division has transferred a guy — call him Mike — to your four-person Agile team. Mike had been dedicated, motivated, energetic, and diligent, but it's been two months and he's not showing those traits. His contribution on your team is only so-so.

Is your team 25% better off by adding this one "resource"? Is his old team proportionally less productive? Are these even the right questions to ask? There are at least two real management issues here. The first is that Mike was willing to dedicate a lot of energy on behalf of his previous division, but that's not happening on your team (or maybe he is really trying to, but your team isn't receptive to him). The other issue is that the team he left hasn't just taken a productivity hit; they have also been set back socially and emotionally in correlation to Mike's stature within that team.

As long as you have people deliver business value, you're going to have to stop counting them. They are not robots or printers or staplers. Their output does not correlate to their input (such as their salary) and it never stays constant. That is even more pronounced in an Agile environment, where people's output also depends on the other team members and their interrelationships. And unlike physical resources, people work for you voluntarily; they may withdraw their consent anytime.

Even if you don't refer to your staff as resources, how do you describe their contribution? In a world filled with such uninspiring titles as "programmer analyst," "HR generalist," and "marketing manager," how do you give them credit?

In some companies, HR staff are called "people people." At Menlo Innovations, business analysts are called "High-Tech Anthropologists" and their goal is "to end human suffering in the world as it relates to technology." Some Agile teams have "team facilitators" instead of ScrumMasters, leaders, or managers.

You can also use plain English to describe what people do to create results. Let's take movie-making, for example. I'm ignorant about it, so the credit roll rarely means anything to me. Except for one family movie,[3] where contributors' names were grouped into the following categories:

+ People in the movie + Stunts, Puppeteers, Stand-ins
+ People who helped MAKE the movie
+ People who followed people with THE CAMERA
+ People who created things that WERE there
+ People who PUT CLOTHES on people
+ People who recorded PEOPLE talking
+ People who made people LOOK good
+ People who made SURE we PAID people
+ People who PUT stuff in the right ORDER
+ People who created THINGS that weren't THERE

Participation

The textbook Agile team has about seven people who assume three roles: customer/product owner, ScrumMaster/team lead, and delivery team. However, the actual cast of characters involved in turning an idea into a product is usually larger than that, and includes managers, stakeholders, sponsors, and sometimes users. This group constantly needs to ask itself: Is everyone giving their best?

In a typical technology organization, there are many barriers to participation and communication. People need approval for certain actions. Development communicates with Operations via a ticketing system. People don't always feel safe expressing needs or risks. Quieter or introverted folks affect decisions less than the talkative or extraverted. Habits, as well as organizational and national culture, may condition Agile teams to take marching orders from "the business" or "management."

> I once led the server development team in an 80-person company. I could strike up a conversation with anyone anytime; but if I wanted to coordinate even a single work item with the client development team, I first had to get my manager to talk to their manager. Thus, every developer in that organization mostly kept to themselves and their small team.

A key Agile belief is that a group can do better than its members working individually. Thus, an Agile environment allows the team's wisdom and positive synergy to emerge. This requires the members to apply themselves; Agile is keen on four principles that remove barriers to participation:

+ **Respect:** honor others' humanity and sense of worth

+ **Trust:** assume others would act professionally and conscientiously

+ **Transparency:** have easy access to the information that guides decisions and actions

+ **Personal safety:** expect no harm or retribution for acting in what you think is the shared interest

These principles amplify one another. Group members who respect each other, trust one another to act professionally, share correct information and context freely, and feel safe from reprisal will *want* to work on their group's goal; they won't merely focus on personal goals. When these principles are present, managers and leads may still expect accountability — to what those individual contributors voluntarily said they'd do. Instead of controlling people, accountability becomes a mechanism to catalyze performance and build relationships.[4]

> A senior developer, highly respected by his peers as well as management, once told me: "They hired me for my Agile skills and experience, but I can't afford to suggest Agile ideas that contradict what my manager says. Do this a few times around here, and you can forget about your annual bonus."

Once people feel free to participate, the Agile mind-set suggests approaches to amplifying individual as well as shared results:

Put people on equal footing. The team uses mechanisms of collaboration and consensus to determine what to do, decide how to do it, and cocreate it. There is no hierarchy inside the ideal Agile team. As well, seniority and experience are good for knowledge, not authority.

Set clear expectations. The team determines their rules of engagement and working agreements. They operate within wide yet well-articulated boundaries. For example, in iteration planning, the product owner may ask for explanations about estimates, but should not discredit them.

Begin with the end in mind. The team concentrates on producing value rather than on tasks and schedules. Every member understands the purpose of each piece of work (its why), not just the mechanics of doing it (its how). Recognizing needs, identifying problems, and solving them together tends to energize people; laying out tasks and making to-do lists rarely has that effect.

Finish together. As a group, team members focus on just a few tasks or needs at a given time. If everyone is scattered doing different things, the result can only be a straight sum of individual contributions.

Emphasize "needle-movers." Leaders and managers acknowledge team members for value delivery, continuous improvement, and taking leadership – not simply for performing assigned tasks.

The team will not succeed together if they don't meet the conditions for participation, as was the case in the following story.

"On a co-located team I was coaching, a developer once got into a shouting match with a business analyst testing his code. Matters quickly got from bad to worse. When the analyst couldn't find me, the product owner, or the ScrumMaster (all three of us were in a meeting), HR was asked to intervene. By the time my meeting ended, the developer had been put on an anger management program and the incident was recorded in a now-tainted personnel record. Witnesses to the event said it wasn't even that bad. The result was that the most productive developer on the team did little work going forward."

– John Hill, Agile Coach and Trainer

Imperfect Humans

At the time of writing this book, most knowledge work is still performed by human beings, not by technology. And every one of those human beings, no matter how intelligent, sensible, and professional, will sometimes:

+ Misunderstand what they are asked to achieve

+ Misinterpret communication

✦ Have their own ideas

✦ Solve and build more than they need to

✦ Lose motivation

✦ Procrastinate

✦ Forget a promise

✦ Make puzzling or questionable decisions

✦ Keep information and suggestions to themselves

✦ Freeze or get stuck

✦ Become overloaded and overwhelmed

✦ Cope, deny, or quit instead of taking responsibility

Rather than pretend these shortcomings don't occur, or fight them with performance improvement plans, or tag the people as "difficult," Agile works with them. One key Agile principle that responds to these shortcomings is to have workers form collaborative teams (more on this in the next chapter). Two other central Agile principles that respond to humans' imperfect nature are to begin with the end in mind and to establish short feedback loops.

We explored the principle "begin with the end in mind" in chapter 2: at every scale, know your context, clarify your outcome, and understand how you will make a difference. This approach is an excellent motivator and source of buy-in and engagement. It galvanizes people to take useful action *and* not to overdo it, because they can tell when they've done enough. Getting to "Done" quickly becomes a habit.

The other principle is to use short feedback loops. Whether working alone or on a team, and on any scale, short feedback loops make up for all the shortcomings listed above. For example:

✦ If a developer misunderstands a story, then a peer review or customer acceptance testing will detect that in short order.

✦ If a team member procrastinates on a work item, gets stuck during its implementation, or overdoes it, that item won't move on the planning board. Anyone watching the board would notice, or the entire team would catch it during the daily meeting.

✦ Since team members interact frequently, they ought to notice when one of their peers loses motivation. They may give feedback about it to that person, or, if they are not comfortable doing so, to the team lead.

Even in organizational cultures that aren't quite human-centric, these three principles alone — form collaborative teams, begin with the end in mind, and use short feedback loops — go a long way to mitigate the risk of employing human beings. In cultures that truly value "individuals and interactions," additional attitudes prevail. While these aren't formally part of the Agile mind-set, they align with it perfectly. Here are some of the better-known ones. Like the principles that enable participation, these attitudes amplify each other.

Assume best intent. If you trust others' competence and professionalism, do so 100%. If one day someone acts strangely, don't jump to conclusions about their qualities or their fit with the team. Instead, assume they had a good reason to act as they did (even if you can't imagine what the reason was). Retrospectives yield better outcomes when the participants agree with this assumption.[5]

Seek forgiveness, not permission. If you feel strongly that a certain novel idea would be valuable, but waiting for an authority's approval would hold up progress, you might act on it — and later take responsibility for your actions.

Failure is okay. A great deal of dysfunctional behavior in organizations is due to fear of failure. As we saw in chapter 2, deliberate failure can be a learning mechanism, but this is different: quite simply, people will sometimes screw up. If we accept them as generally competent professionals, and if they take responsibility for their actions, then they never have to fear failure. They'll think of it as learning and feedback, and feel free to do the right thing.

Live with the consequences of your actions. If you produce code that has a defect, who will have to fix it — you, a colleague in your team, or someone in another country charged with "sustaining engineering"? If you design overly coupled product architecture, who will have to disentangle unneeded dependencies during implementation? In stable, cross-functional teams (which is the Agile preference), people know that they *will* have to reckon with today's decisions at some point.

If doing something hurts, do it more often. People often put off activities they expect to be painful (the popular candidates in technology development being integration and deployment). But the more they put them off, the more the work accumulates and the greater the pain: a vicious cycle. By contrast, carrying out the activity in smaller doses, more often, may take the pain away, or may numb you to it as it becomes habit.

An example of a practice that manifests all the above is continuous deployment. In organizations that employ this practice, every developer may release code into production almost any time, resulting in potentially dozens of deployments per day. This technical practice makes possible very rapid feedback loops that support business decisions. However, it has business and cultural consequences: some deployments *will* fail, certain experiments *will* bomb, and technical problems *might* cost business. Some organizations that practice it successfully will accompany it with blameless retrospectives and incident investigations, to which everyone is invited. For them, "failure" is an opportunity for all hands to learn about their systems and how to work together.[6]

Frequent Accomplishments

A week before writing this section of the book, I participated in my first-ever 5-kilometer running race and achieved a personal record: 31 minutes.

A couple of years earlier, I didn't run at all. In the first few weeks of training, I still considered running unpleasant, even a punishment (due to some high school experiences). My motivation to run was high, but 5km seemed quite theoretical. To make it realistic, I set interim goals. The first was to run 1.5km. Then it was to run 15 minutes. Then 20 minutes. Then 4km. And finally the race.

Accomplishing an interim goal made subsequent ones less theoretical and daunting. I learned that I could, in fact, run. I grew proud of myself. I discovered that running can be exhilarating — quite the opposite of punishment. Those goals had specific meaning to me, and each step was just one more little commitment.

Applying this thinking to large development efforts has similar effects. While six- or 18-month projects might be considered ordinary, for most people that is too long to wait for feedback about how useful their efforts are. It's not enough to craft a compelling project vision, nor is it enough to have an end in mind; rather, frequent accomplishments are needed to keep people engaged and productive — to make them care.

Traditional methods have their own accomplishments. These are called milestones, and they usually occur several months apart. Some milestones have to do with a subgroup of the project community achieving its own goal, such as "specification ready" and "code complete." A good deal of time and effort go into accomplishing those goals, so "frequent" they are not.

Accomplishments in Agile are different: they are bigger than the individual or subgroup — they belong to the entire team — and they have to do with making a tangible difference. Thus, populating a product backlog might be an early milestone, but it's not a motivation-enhancing interim goal. The canonical example of an Agile accomplishment is releasing a product increment and having customers accept it. There are other examples, however; as long as the environment truly supports the Agile values, the likelihood of having frequent accomplishments is high.

Sustainable Pace

"Crunch time." "Heads down." "We're down to the wire." "Everyone's working evenings and weekends." "The client is getting nervous." This is the language of the last few days, weeks, and sometimes months of a major Waterfall development effort. That period also has its subculture, such as takeout dinners in the office, heroic solutions and workarounds, and urgent emails at 3 a.m.

This situation is still considered normal in some places. Team members bear part of the cost: their families are affected, some of them experience burnout, and most never get paid fairly for the overtime. The business bears another part of the cost through higher management overhead and labor-related expenses. There are also hidden costs: the quality of overtime work isn't stellar, everyone needs a recovery period after "the crunch," and some people just decide not to bother anymore — they leave. (Euphemistically, they "move on.")

A proper Agile environment neutralizes many of the conditions that give rise to these scenarios. Iterative planning, regular and quick feedback, collaboration, and a focus on value and outcome within well-articulated constraints all help to keep the team on track and prevent "scope creep" and late surprises. But that's only process. Agile has an explicit people-centric principle in this regard, and it's not optional: everyone involved should work at a *sustainable pace*.

Every person works at a certain pace: some measure of his or her capacity to work productively. A team working together also has a pace. A person or team operating at a *sustainable* pace is able to perform for a long time without sacrifice, particularly of personal well-being and of their deliverable's quality. Their pace may fluctuate occasionally (for instance around holidays). All things being equal, people who work at a sustainable pace retain their morale, motivation, and clear thinking.

Working without sufficient rest is known to degrade performance and cause increased mistakes in diverse fields, such as emergency medicine, long-distance driving, and the military. Despite having a built-in social support structure, Agile teams are no better off. I have seen more than enough examples of an unsustainable pace hurting teamwork and collaboration: the stressed members resorted to blame and guilt, focused only on their own needs, and lost empathy toward colleagues.

What passes for "sustainable" is highly specific to the team or the person. It has to do with the number of work hours in a week, but also with organizational culture, personal expectations, and motivation. Every team needs to discover the best pace they can sustain. Their planning activities take into account their productivity (output capacity) at that pace. Using the continuous improvement principle, they find ways to increase their productivity while working at that pace. The principles of trust and respect are critical for supporting this dynamic.

In Agile, overtime and heroics are exceptions because they are both risky and unsustainable. Part of continuous reflection and adjustment is to find ways to minimize overtime and heroics. The goal is to make the team a true organizational asset, one that produces reliably over the long term.

In 2002–2003, I led the bioinformatics group in a structure-guided drug discovery company. We were responsible for small- and large-scale software development, tool integration, and data management and analysis. We kept our software customers happy with collaborative planning and solid upgrades every few weeks. Over those two years, our process — heavy on Extreme Programming practices[7] — was so reliable that we never had to work nights or weekends.

Slack and Utilization

Let's say you are used to working 40 hours per week, and can sustain this pace for months. You always find enough useful tasks to keep you busy, and you carry them out productively. Should you fill up all your time with those tasks?

Many teams do exactly that; this approach is known as maximizing utilization (of the team's so-called "resources"). People also do that in their personal lives; when my twins were very young, it felt like all my nonwork waking hours went to parenting. Many of this book's readers routinely set aside a portion of their personal time on evenings and weekends to catch up on work.

Even if you use all your time and energy productively, you're still giving something up. That something is the opportunities you didn't know about when you made plans for that time. They are opportunities to *change* something: improve capabilities, get away with a simpler solution, innovate, even reconsider the plan. (As John Lennon wrote in "Beautiful Boy," "Life is what happens to you while you're busy making other plans.")

Opportunities don't care for your iteration backlogs or your strategy meetings. Opportunities don't always make themselves clearly noticeable, either. Taking advantage of them is sometimes difficult when you already have your work cut out for you.

If opportunities to change are important to you in a given context, you can make it easier to notice them, and to reckon with them, by incorporating slack[8] in your process. Slack is that extra time you set aside for thinking about the work, especially creative or complex work. It is a deliberate attempt to expand your mind, to consider more inputs and ideas, and to amplify learning. It is not a buffer you reserve for crunch time, unplanned work, or underestimated commitments. Every week, no matter how busy I am, I schedule a couple of opportunities for my personal favorite form of slack: taking a long walk.

Agile retrospectives are a form of structured slack: on a regular basis, the team takes time to reflect on their process and teamwork. Going offsite for training or attending conferences is a learning-oriented form of slack. Pairing with a teammate on a task lets both of you have unstructured slack: while one types or writes, the other can think. These are only three examples of making learning and change possible.

In a healthy Agile environment, people feel respected and appreciated. There are few barriers to their participation. Folks *want* to work on the goals of their group, which accepts their sometimes-less-than-perfect behavior. They have frequent accomplishments while working at a sustainable pace, and they keep spare bandwidth for noticing opportunities, innovating, and thinking about change. Still, they don't usually work alone. In the next chapter, we'll see the Agile perspective on teams.

Chapter 5
Performing as a Team

The Agile approach to determining and planning the work applies even when the whole team is a single person. In most product development situations nowadays, however, a single person is not enough. The traditional way to organize multiple workers is to create hierarchies and functional groups. Agile prefers networks of flat, semi-autonomous, and cross-functional teams. Having explored the Agile view of the individual, let's explore its values, beliefs, and principles around putting people in teams.

Rights

As the previous chapters explained, Agile places a premium on completing valuable work frequently, and is practically obsessed with it. The unit that accomplishes that — turning ideas into shippable increments — is the team. In fact, the sole reason an Agile team comes together is to deliver value to their customers in support of business objectives.

In order to get to "Done," the team must include people with the necessary skills and qualities, who must be as present and available as possible. This is a source of tension in many companies, because it implies that certain members may not reach their maximum potential *output*. This implication is real, but the popular reaction to it — that extra capacity is wasteful and ought to be put to productive use — is not helpful. Optimizing any person's or function's busy time jeopardizes *the team's ability* to complete deliverables frequently. Since too much extra capacity isn't economical, teams and managers always need to balance responsiveness with efficiency in their particular situation.

Having the potential to deliver value (by having appropriate skills and qualities) is not enough. An Agile team is semiautonomous, having certain rights that enable it to be effective:

✦ Only the team may commit itself to produce a certain set of outcomes in a given time frame. (Many organizations have discovered that managers' committing on teams' behalf doesn't always yield good results.)

✦ The team self-organizes around the work: only they determine which members will do the work and how they will do it. They don't have to wait for an authority to tell them that. In fact, there is no expectation of hierarchy, or even a reporting relationship, within a team. There is also no expectation that roles stay fixed over time. In advanced teams, the lines separating roles may be rather blurry.

✦ If the team has a problem, such as an impediment to work flow, the team is empowered and expected to notice it and respond to it: solve it, request assistance, or escalate it.

A team is typically one unit inside a larger entity: the organization. Two additional rights in this context are:

- ✦ The team decides how to improve itself and its capabilities. It should do so in support of the organization's interests, plans, and needs. The team should feel free to request assistance from management, but continuous improvement is the team's responsibility, not someone else's.

- ✦ The team has the right to know their boundaries and success criteria, as well as management's expectations.

These rights make some managers nervous. Others may roll their eyes and say, "What a nice socialist utopia." Teams may not be too comfortable with these rights, either. This relationship between managers and teams — you deliver, we'll support and empower you — removes a sense of predictability and control that both parties might be used to.

> My team actually told me they are "afraid of being yelled at for making a wrong decision."
>
> – *Jack Wendel, Agile/Lean Evangelist, Conceptual Performance*

Endowing a team with these rights aligns with modern management thinking of moving decision-making about the work closer to the workers. This is good because workers have the most accurate and current information about *their* work. This approach reduces the risk of making managers single points of failure. And the resulting human systems are more resilient to change (change being not only a constant, but something that Agile harnesses for competitive advantage).

There is a catch, however. A team can apply these rights only if it is, in fact, a team. It is a team when it has a goal that is larger than individual goals, when it requires all members, and when none of them can claim individual victory until it is done.[1] In a proper team, members don't have individual product-related goals; they have shared goals and individual growth goals. They win together or they lose together. They are accountable to each other, not only to their manager. They work through their inevitable conflicts. This requires trust and a suitable social environment, so that members want to be good to each other, honor their personal commitments, and moderate their behaviors.

Most teams don't exceed 10 members.[2] If the work requires more people, it might be beneficial to organize into two or more related teams. Every one of those teams enjoys the rights described above. This group of teams must have a compelling common identity, which relates to the value they collectively deliver. When the members have allegiance both to their own small team and to the larger community, they eschew the "our team did our part" trap, and enable the entire community to complete valuable work.

Shared Responsibility

A popular business concept suggests seeing staff as more than producers: they are "owners." That's good for business because owners *care*. Owners seize opportunities to create results. They uphold values and take responsibility. While not everyone has legal ownership shares, the discourse is very much about everyone being in it together and treating their products and artifacts as if they owned them.

The Agile style of teamwork — everyone caring about getting valuable items to completion — pushes a lot of project management-type work onto the team. The team *owns its progress*; this matter is no longer concentrated in the hands of a team lead, manager, or project manager.

Unfortunately, many people in organizations don't act as if they *own* their product, but rather as if they *rent* it. In programming, examples of renter behaviors include:

+ Building unsound or poorly designed code

+ Turning a blind eye to a potential defect

+ Leaving "to-do" comments in the code
+ Considering items done after only basic acceptance testing
+ Investing too little in maintenance

Both the ownership and rental attitudes arise from organizational culture. *Telling* people to consider themselves "owners" (together with their colleagues) is not enough. An organization that tries to embrace the Agile mind-set without cultivating an ownership attitude probably will not prosper.

The Agile mind-set exacts a higher standard than ownership, expecting team members to also share *responsibility*. The idea is that all members look after what's important in their particular team, including their output, decisions, and process. Even though each member may contribute only a piece of any given result, the team shares responsibility for outcomes achieved (or missed!) by any of its members. The self-organization mechanism is critical for shared responsibility.

In an Agile transformation I supported a few years ago, the team experienced a common pattern: the developers were outpacing the testers. By the end of the second iteration, the three testers (two of whom were new) were staring up a mountain of work. At the retrospective, the developers agreed to shift much of their efforts to testing, so *the team* could finish all outstanding work. Indeed, during the next iteration, the "Done" column grew rapidly, and only a few new items were added to "ready for testing." One of the programmers, unprompted, took particular charge; every day, he paired up with the testers, helping them set up more quickly and contributing useful information.

The potential for shared responsibility is bounded by the level of shared ownership. Yet once ownership is there, shared responsibility is easy to bring about. It is a good motivator: we succeed together when I've got your back and you've got mine. The cross-functional, self-organizing nature of the team is a powerful and consistent signal that members are in it together. High levels of visibility and transparency encourage everyone to do good work and truly care about shared objectives. Shared responsibility, in turn, reinforces all these elements: it is a virtuous cycle.

Nevertheless, it's also easy to destroy shared responsibility. This is particularly evident in organizations that don't realize (or don't accept) that an Agile team self-organizes to *complete* work quickly. In their daily standup meetings, instead of having a team conversation about progress toward their shared commitment, individuals place a greater emphasis on *their own* contribution ("my part's done"), what *they* are planning to do, and what's holding *them* up. This presumes individual rather than shared responsibility.

In a functionally organized environment, a worker finishes her piece and throws it over the metaphorical wall to the next function in the process. Analysts throw specifications to developers, who in turn throw code builds to QA, and so forth. In the cross-functional Agile team, members may specialize and may pass partial work around, but all of them share responsibility for its completion. They may collaborate on it, for instance by pairing or "swarming"; people may take extra time to explain their understanding and thoughts; they may review work for one another. If a deliverable is not completed, it's everybody's concern, not the fault of the person who last held the ball.

Regardless of the organizational culture, shared responsibility is voluntary. In the previous story, everyone helped finish open items, but one of the developers was visibly reluctant to do so. She was a highly competent programmer, and believed that her time was better spent moving items from "Scheduled" to "Dev Done," not to later stages. In fact, one day during the third iteration she told me, "They pay me quite a lot to do that kind of work [testing]."

Learning

For a team to deliver appropriate products, they must learn a lot about their business, industry, and technology. Since these keep changing, the team never stops learning about them. Fortunately, this is mostly factual learning. (The many established ways by which individuals and teams engage in it are outside the scope of this book.)

For a team to reach a high level of effectiveness and maintain it, they must also learn about the consequences of their decisions and actions. For instance, was a certain technical implementation choice a good idea? Was the decision to deploy an early version helpful or a mistake? They must also learn about their abilities and limitations, how to work together, and how they respond to change.

This type of learning depends on useful feedback loops. It is amplified when the entire team contributes to the feedback and handles it collaboratively. Scrum, the popular Agile framework, prescribes two such learning opportunities at the end of each sprint (iteration). In the first meeting, called the Review, the team and stakeholders inspect the iteration's product increment in order to adapt it. In the second, the Retrospective, the team inspects and adapts how they work together. Both meetings are a deliberate pause from product construction, a form of slack (see chapter 4) to concentrate the team's thinking on what they had chosen to do, what they actually did, and how to do better. Efficient learning contributes to effective value delivery. Teams that keep their cost of change low can welcome the learning.

Teams may review their product increment anytime they want, if they expect to learn something useful. The same goes for the retrospective, which does not have to be a big ceremony or be confined to the end of a cycle. For instance, teams may convene a special retrospective after a production outage or a member's departure.

Given the number and diversity of participants, these meetings — and other learning opportunities — need facilitation. Facilitation turns a retrospective from group discussion to structured discovery, one that results in action (and doesn't wither due to silence or get hijacked by dominant personalities). Skilled facilitation affords a team the safety and support to discuss sensitive matters — and every team I've ever known made great strides once they allowed themselves to discuss matters beyond the obvious and the superficial.

> The 15 members of the new "Data Team" gathered for their second iteration retrospective. They had been struggling with teamwork due to a culture of individual accomplishments and their divergent and imbalanced skill set. Instead of the basic free-form process of asking "What Worked Well?" and "What Could Be Improved?" my coaching partner and I picked a specific question for the retro:
>
> "How can we better support one another to get work to 'Done' more effectively?"
>
> I took the team through the highly collaborative facilitation technique known as the Consensus Workshop.[3] Everybody contributed, the energy was high, and they stayed on track throughout the hour. The team left with four actionable ideas and experiments, all different from the *visible* elements of teamwork that had preoccupied them: standup meetings and planning boards.

The Agile team is in charge of its own learning. Some teams don't know how to carry out that charge efficiently, and some teams don't do it enough. This is particularly evident in teams that are pressured to perform (whether subtly or explicitly), and thus keep themselves busy just knocking items off a backlog. Such a team can use a recognized leader, who regularly reminds the team of the need to learn and constantly supports it in making that happen.

Teams are not limited to prescheduled learning opportunities, although that is convenient. A habit of growth-minded individuals and teams is to reflect on a situation that recently ended and ask themselves, "What could we learn from that?" One example is iteration planning in summertime, which is often considered a headache because every week a different set of people is absent. But absences are normal; there are merely more of them in summertime. Rather than forgo process or remain blocked on most work, a team might use this constraint as a learning catalyst to increase its resilience.

Collaboration

The Agile team is the unit that produces value. Its members manage their own work and they learn continuously. Yet that is not enough: a team might fulfill these expectations and still be just a group of people who meet frequently, divide up the work, and reconvene at the end of the iteration. Teams may grow to be far more productive than the sum of their individual contributions if they employ one more principle from the Agile mind-set: collaboration.

Collaboration means working together on a task and sharing responsibility for the outcome. It requires shared understanding — which is a state, not a statement. It requires a basic level of generalism and cross-training. It is different from cooperation, in which every participant takes care of their own part with the hope of a win-win outcome. People may collaborate in various forms, and they might not divide the work equally at all — their guiding principle is to produce a valuable outcome together. Collaboration cannot take place without respect and trust, whereas cooperation may happen without them.

Having the people who define value (such as product owners) communicate and collaborate closely with those who produce it (such as developers and testers) is an Obviously Good Thing, so it occurs in many Agile teams. The diverse perspectives and knowledge areas of these two roles — the former is typically business, the latter is typically technology — enable all parties to identify the right value to deliver and find mutually useful solutions.

However, in the Agile philosophy, collaboration may (and often should) take place among any group of workers, not just across roles. A pervasive belief among many software developers — and I suppose also among other knowledge workers — causes them to miss this point: they believe that trained, experienced professionals ought to be able to complete tasks well all by themselves, therefore their colleagues may have little to contribute to the result. Moreover, bringing those colleagues on to the task to make their small contribution is viewed as a waste of time, considering what they already have on their plates.

This belief ignores a very good reason for collaboration: that team members are human. As we saw in the previous chapter, even the most professional and conscientious workers are not perfect "resources." Having people work in collaborative teams mitigates the human fallibilities that affect them when working solo. Simply put, a member of an Agile team never has to struggle alone. He or she can ask teammates for help or feedback. They can notice when their colleague procrastinates, freezes, or gets overloaded, and can respond to that. If someone is stuck and thereby jeopardizes the team's promises, helping the stuck person may be more important than having others make their own progress.

The flexible nature of Agile is often touted as an enabler of innovation. Yet teams cannot innovate if they just put "must haves" on the backlog and if members maximize their individual work time consuming that backlog. In appendix B, the "Unscripted Collaboration" section tells a personal story of collaboration as a source of innovation.

Alas, the foregoing statements — that team members ask for help, and that others respond when they see evidence of personal struggle — do not always stand the test of reality. Most people (at least those I get to meet — and remember I'm paid to show up and help them do better) just don't ask for help nearly enough. Worse, they feel uncomfortable giving each other feedback. That is why several practices have emerged to remove the associated discomfort and anxiety. Here are some examples:

✦ Co-location, that is, inhabiting a shared space. Better yet, the workspace is small enough that every member can see and hear the others. Beyond the obvious benefit of face-to-face communication, such a workspace removes a common barrier to collaboration: distance. The distance between two people has to be *very* small for one of them to get out of his chair and walk over to the other person.

✦ No-exceptions pairing: no team member ever performs a task alone. (The pairs rotate and switch frequently to increase diversity and reduce risk.)

✦ When a number of teams are involved, let people coordinate through already-existing "small world networks" in addition to going through designated leads and contacts.

✦ Make useful team information easily accessible, such as by putting it on the wall near a team. Information that boosts collaboration is about the team's goal, agreements about working together, their progress, and risks/impediments to flow.

✦ Use collaborative techniques in team meetings, such as planning and retrospectives.

SUPPLEMENTARY RESOURCE: Download the "Pairing Do's and Don't's" poster from the book's companion website, **www.TheAgileMindsetBook.info**.

Servant Leadership

Agile teams are expected to self-organize, learn together, and collaborate. However, they are not like this from day one. Teams evolve through three stages — Forming, Storming, and Norming — on the way to the desired stage, Performing, in which collaboration and positive synergy yield greater performance than the sum of individual contributions.[4] long the way, which takes months, the organization in which they operate exerts various forces on them. Many of those forces aren't helpful to team evolution; examples include deadline pressures, process and tool dictation, micromanagement, and staffing changes. *A team's success is not inevitable.*

To reach the Norming stage, and to graduate out of it to Performing, teams need leadership. Every member has some level of innate leadership that may help their team prosper. However, a vast majority of technical teams benefit from dedicated leadership: the Agile team leader.

An Agile team leader (ATL) is a special case of the servant leader: a leader whose primary goal is to develop her followers as they accomplish the team goal. The ATL points out the team's direction and clarifies the context and boundary in which they operate. The ATL supports individuals' growth through feedback, reflection, and coaching. She helps the team be a team, for instance by facilitating team interactions, creating shared understanding, and acting as their process steward. The ATL helps identify and resolve conflicts, sometimes acting as a pressure valve for team members. The ATL helps the team notice and remove impediments to their flow. And, as needed, she protects the team from undue organizational pressure.

Effective Agile leaders do all that without *requiring* formal authority (even though in many organizations they also happen to be managers). In fact, positional authority may be a hindrance because of the temptation to command and control others. A prime example of this temptation is when problems arise. In the Agile mind-set, teams should solve their own problems; their leader may assist them, but should not step in and tackle the problems on their behalf. For instance, instead of responding to a team-level problem with "Give me options" or "Tell me what to do," a leader would "take it to the team" for a conversation and a decision.

Agile leaders and managers make it a personal goal to support their teams' performance and nurture their well-being. To achieve this goal, they'll sometimes rely on others' feedback and advice, however uncomfortable they may be.

Every now and then, I receive the following type of request: "My team seems to do well, but they seem a bit stuck and we're unsure of what to change. Could you check us out and suggest improvements?" Before they sign on, I explain that I'll consider not only the team, but also the relationships and interactions they have with their management — including the person who contracts me.

When we eventually meet to review my analysis and suggestions, some of those managers admit: "I was quite nervous going into this assessment; I was worried what you'd find that *I* was doing wrong. But I went ahead with it because I wanted my team to do better."

The first value of Agile is to put people before process. This does not require leaders who act all touchy-feely or treat staff with kid gloves. It doesn't mean democracy or communism, either. The servant leadership principle means creating an environment where people feel free and safe to do great work and make their team better.

"As a manager you have to avoid being a gatekeeper or a bottleneck. It can result in tremendous inefficiencies. If you step back and support your team, hold your breath for a little bit, you'll be amazed at what a self-organized team can do. Based on this learning alone there's a lot that's changed about my job."

– Eugene Kiel, Vice President at Cengage Learning

Stability

The cross-functional nature of Agile teams, not to mention their association with a certain value stream, may remind you of matrix management. If your company is moving to Agile from a functional hierarchy using traditional methods, the first few teams might in fact operate in a matrix environment. There is, however, a significant difference between matrixing as commonly practiced and Agile, and it has to do with a team's longevity.

Typically, a matrix organization takes a "push" approach: when there's important work to do, a team is assembled to carry it out. The team is "pushed" onto the job. By contrast, Agile follows Lean thinking in taking a "pull" approach: standing teams pull work from a queue of important initiatives, often called "the project portfolio" or some variation on "backlog."

Both approaches get the work done. Both also address the inevitable need to handle urgent work: in "push," people are removed from their teams to form a new project team or task force; in "pull," a team stops what it's doing and switches to the urgent task. An Agile team is set up for responsiveness — it never has too many or too large work items in flight — so a pull approach is not terribly disruptive. Moreover, since the team remains unchanged in the process, its level of performance isn't likely to suffer much. By contrast, a "push" team starts fresh, and its members' former teams get knocked down to Storming, where their performance is much lower.

Agile teams prefer to stay together over the long haul, which may be years. Over time they amass responsibilities; it's not uncommon to see long-standing teams in charge of several systems, products, and tools. Stability allows them to maximize learning; their knowledge is a critical asset to the organization, since much of it is tacit and undocumented (or not usefully documentable). They build shared history and retain organizational memory. And for many people, the team at work becomes a second family or community, which keeps them motivated and engaged long after the excitement factor of the business and the technology has subsided.

Agile teams are considerably different from traditional manager-run teams of "resources." They have a considerable measure of autonomy and shared responsibility, they learn and collaborate, and the environment supports their growth. Most managers and individual contributors have little experience with this construct.

For extensive guidance on the practicalities of Agile servant leadership, all the way from forming teams through supporting their self-organization and cultivating their Agility, read my 2012 book, *The Human Side of Agile*.

The next chapter examines the concept of technical Agility: the *doing* of work in an Agile manner.

Chapter 6
Doing the Work, Part I

You have a cross-functional, collaborative team whose purpose is to deliver value (chapter 5). The team works at a sustainable pace, it maintains slack, and its members participate willingly (chapter 4). They have feedback and decision-making mechanisms for determining what to deliver (chapter 2) as well as methods for planning the work (chapter 3). They are starting their next iteration, for which they've planned a certain set of deliverables. How will they go about doing the work? And how can they ensure a high level of *technical Agility* — that they are executing the value-adding mechanics of the work with Agility?

In most Agile implementations, the first question is met with the naive answer, "The team self-organizes to meet their commitments." The second question is also met with a textbook answer: "They will regularly use feedback and data to trigger process improvements." These answers are correct, but superficial — so superficial, in fact, that many teams don't realize what liabilities they've incurred (in quick iterations) until it's too late. The consequences of insufficient technical Agility are dire: within a few months, Agile planning and teamwork falters, and the team's ability to innovate and respond falls behind.

This chapter explores the values, beliefs, and principles of technical Agility. And if you're interested in software development, the next chapter expands the picture of technical Agility to that field.

Progressing

Traditional management theory calls for managing the *workers*. Managers have to keep them busy performing their job duties, because they are expensive. This thinking dates back to factory management, where idle resources (such as machinery) were costly. Agile, on the other hand, calls for managing the *work*, and for taking care of the workers. This perspective is not just about efficiency in task management; it's also about making sure that work gets done. In healthy Agile environments, people trust each other to act on shared interests.

Since, in Agile, finishing deliverables early and frequently is important, the unit that turns ideas into shippable increments — the team — needs to keep the work moving. They move it all the way to completion, since working product is the primary measure of progress. Keeping every member *busy* is at most a secondary consideration.

Every time I teach the Agile fundamentals, I explain that however long an iteration takes, a team focuses on getting items to *"Done"*: what they produce *works*. It's tested, solid, and potentially deployable; it doesn't just look-sort-of-okay on someone's computer. Even after 10 years of teaching, I still get this type of response:

"Seriously? You mean, tested and all? *Done-done?*"

Sometimes this is accompanied by nervous shifting in seats. Other times I catch a snickering look of the "yeah, right" variety. Occasionally I see a genuine oh-dear-what-am-I-getting-myself-into stare. So I explain further: the idea is to meet the team's definition of "Done," which is presumably fairly expansive (see chapter 3). Getting to "Done" supports what Agile practitioners hold important: value delivery and responding to change. Those students, however, are still viewing the world from a different mind-set:

+ They value giving users complete solutions. Therefore, they believe that unless a deliverable is sizable, it can't be valuable.

+ They believe that making meaningful changes to previously built increments requires weeks of regression testing (to make sure nothing broke).

+ They want to minimize time and effort. If the next feature is understood, they reason, let's just develop it straightaway, not in small pieces. They also assign work to task experts, believing they'll do it the best and fastest.

+ Developers believe they never have enough time to code.

+ Testers believe they never have enough time to test.

As we saw in chapter 1, people's values and beliefs inform their choice of principles and methods. The all-too-common set quoted above gives rise to the misperception that a 10-day iteration ought to include six days of building surrounded by one day of planning, two days of testing, and one day of stabilization — in other words, a mini-Waterfall. Teams that equate iterations with mini-Waterfalls experience mini-consequences, such as programmers and testers having a mini-death-march every two weeks.

But hang on, if we're not planning to deliver value until at least the end of the iteration, *why not* minimize time and effort and thereby possibly produce a more complete solution?

The reason, again, has to do with one of the four values: adaptation. You might value adaptation (also called responsiveness) so much that it would make sense to allow it throughout the iteration, not just at its boundaries. For instance, if you discover a promising opportunity or a gnarly problem during development, should you file it away for later consideration, or respond to it? If midway through working on a promised feature you learn that another feature *must* take precedence now, will you be able to switch quickly, and what will you do with the work in progress? If halfway through a three-day task you discover that it's really a six-day task, should you keep going, rethink the plan, or work overtime? If each team member starts working on their specialty and they integrate the parts at the end, what will you do if subsequent testing uncovers high-severity defects?

These questions do not have a universal yes-or-no answer. Their relevance depends on context, team skills, project constraints, stakeholder expectations, and the desired outcome from the time-box. If the questions barely apply, you might produce a detailed iteration plan and simply work that plan. If these are the last few days before a time-sensitive product release, then a detailed, efficiency-minded plan may be precisely the right response. Most Agile teams, in most contexts, do find these questions relevant, however, and pick one of two approaches:

1. Have a detailed plan, and disrupt it if necessary. When replanning, they choose items to fit the remainder of the time-box. Usually, this means removing low-priority items from the planned list.

2. Decompose (split) the deliverables into smaller valuable deliverables, and complete them one, two, or three at a time. If work turns out to take longer than estimated, split some of the planned items into even smaller ones, and complete what's possible within the time-box.

Common to both approaches is the drive to always finish what's started, and always be close to finishing. The item being finished needs to be valuable — but it doesn't have to be big to be valuable.

Many Agile teams measure the magnitude of work they can complete in an iteration, which allows them to make longer-term forecasts. In low-trust environments, these capacity measures take on an additional purpose: checking or proving how busy the team is. The following story has a happy ending; unfortunately, not all teams fare this way.

"The product owner came to me in a panic, having learned that the feature an engineer was working on was no longer needed. Still, he wanted the engineer to finish so that we could claim credit for finishing it. I asked what the value would be in finishing work that was known to be unnecessary. He quickly saw my point and agreed to ask the engineer to stop work on that feature."

– Grace, Agile Coach

Finishing without Delay

Caring about completing valuable work early and frequently gives rise to certain beliefs and principles. Since it's people who complete the work, and they need a process for doing that, one of those principles is to organize the people and design their process to minimize delays. Agile is particularly averse to delays in getting feedback, learning, and delivering value. Hence, some of its response mechanisms to typical product development delays are:

✦ Any person whose contribution is vital to work completion is considered part of the team.

I have known several software teams that consisted solely of programmers and testers, but depended on remote teams of database experts for nontrivial database work. They could not produce feedback-worthy features as quickly as they could if they had a database expert on the team, even if only at 50% capacity.

✦ Team members sit in close quarters to make communication and collaboration easier. They can easily ask each other questions, offer and receive help, and share important information.

A team in an open space

✦ The product owner, who speaks for the users and the business, is expected to be available to answer questions about the current increment. (Those questions typically relate to decisions whose last responsible moment has arrived.) He is also empowered to accept or reject it. This kind of validation or sign-off is quick and informal.

✦ A software development team creates rapid automated tests, which they can run anytime to detect breakage.

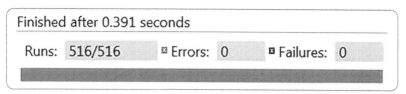

Sample run of a unit test suite

+ Teams establish various mechanisms for coordinating progress, noticing problems, and dealing with them quickly. Popular examples are holding a brief daily meeting and posting the iteration plan visibly.

Sample iteration task board

+ When planning work for an iteration, teams don't try to use up every hour of every member's time. Instead, they reserve some buffer (context-dependent and person-dependent) for helping out, inevitable rework and back-and-forth, and dealing with surprises. By planning for less new stuff and leaving some room for dealing with the unplanned, they are better able to truly get to "Done" on already started items.

Even with proper organization and process, a team may experience impediments to flow. These impediments may be due to technical
problems, organizational limitations, or anything to do with the team's
being human, such as faulty communication.[1] An Agile team is always
on the lookout for impediments, which they attempt to remove forthwith. Many teams benefit from having one person pay extra attention
to such obstacles and lead the charge on their removal; that is the
Agile team leader we encountered in the previous chapter.

Iterations tend to be short, typically a couple of weeks long.
There are obvious business reasons for that, such as adaptation and
feedback, but there's also a human-centric principle at play: focus. In
each iteration, the team only needs to focus on finishing one small
fraction of their overall obligations. This focus helps them get their
heads around work that can otherwise be quite large, complex, or
simply overwhelming.

In many teams, even a two-week-long iteration still amounts to
several features or capabilities and a bunch of small tasks. In recent
years, teams have discovered that applying the focus principle *also at
the item level* helps them get to "Done" more efficiently. By deliberately
putting a *low* limit on the number of items they take on — their "work
in process" (WIP) — they complete valuable, feedback-worthy items
on a more even keel. This deliberate focus has two additional benefits:

1. It prevents teams' natural tendency (especially those teams
    used to individual task assignments) to start all the tasks at
    the same time, which often means some of them are not fin-
    ished at the end of the iteration.

2. It creates a virtuous cycle: a chain of events that reinforce
    themselves and create a positive outcome. Rather than wait
    to the end, team members get an early sense of accomplish-
    ment — even if they only finish one thing from the plan.
    That sense of accomplishment increases their motivation and
    engagement, which encourages them to continue focusing on
    just a handful of items and to bring them to completion.

Limiting the focus to fewer items than there are team members is sometimes good for encouraging collaboration. This may be quite a challenge in highly specialized knowledge work, for instance in scientific research. The distribution of expertise may be such that for some tasks, having two people collaborate slows them both down more than it makes them effective. However, repeatedly assigning work to task experts only perpetuates the siloing problem, and may overload them to the extent of creating bottlenecks. Such teams would do well to frequently assess how their skills distribution supports accomplishing their purpose.

As mentioned in chapter 3, iterations are helpful only if they are disturbance-free. With the self-imposed WIP limit constraint, team members prevent outsiders from causing excessive context switching, and they avoid interrupting *themselves*. Yet they don't work in a vacuum; their environment needs to allow them to focus on the work chosen for the iteration. Even though Agile embraces change, change mid-iteration is disruptive. To the extent possible, teams expect to introduce change — whether based on external feedback or their own new ideas — between iterations. During the iteration, they push back on change whose cost is higher than its value; having a WIP limit reduces the cost of change of items that have not been started yet. The longer an iteration gets, the harder it is to push back justifiably, which is why iterations tend to be only a couple of weeks long.

Quality

Quality is a major factor in the value you deliver to your customer. How do you create quality products?

The Waterfall mind-set associates quality closely with testing. The working assumption is that the right time to test an artifact is after it's produced. The entire team might test requirements; developers test designs, sometimes by creating a proof of concept; testers check the developers' code. Testers might get an early start by thinking through their test plans, but they only execute them after the construction step. "Test-after" doesn't only seem like the logical thing to do, it fits the efficiency expectation of sequential methods: if we specify, design, and build the complete solution to the best of our ability, then a single, comprehensive test pass should suffice.

While the theory makes sense, it meets some challenges in practice. Being the last step in a process squeezes testing for time. Making best efforts in the specify, design, and build stages is never good enough, otherwise testing would be redundant. There is no knowing how many problems would surface during testing. Some of those problems arise from work done in early stages, and fixing them is costly and perhaps too late. To top it all, most testers can only point out problems, not fix them; being bearers of bad news doesn't encourage others to consider them "part of the team." (Remember from chapter 2 that feedback is like going to the doctor?)

Agile has a different approach, which is congruent with the Context-Driven Testing school of thought.[2] The Agile preference for effectiveness over efficiency means that testing is primarily a learning activity, not a confirmatory activity (that would be "checking"). People test products and artifacts by asking questions, making observations, and applying diverse tools in order to uncover helpful information. The underlying principle is continuous quality: quality needs to be present throughout the value stream — from idea through delivered product — and the team needs efficient feedback loops to keep a good handle on their product's quality. Frequent and rapid testing provides information for these feedback loops, answering questions such as:

+ How valuable is what we've built?

+ Who else might use this and in what ways?

+ How easy is it to understand and use?

+ What have we broken along the way?

+ What else does it do that we didn't anticipate?

The value of this feedback diminishes quickly the longer we wait to receive it and apply it, which is why most teams' definition of "Done" includes some variation on the condition "the item has been tested and all significant problems have been fixed."

A key Agile belief is that collaboration mitigates human risk. Thus, the continuous quality principle further states that quality is everyone's concern throughout the process. Any team member may test the product; testers merely specialize. In software teams that have fewer testers than they need, it's not uncommon to see developers engage in testing activities. A developer may pair up with a tester at the beginning of a complex task, as their collaboration may affect the developer's approach.

The Broken Windows theory[3] posits that people interpret visible disrepair and vandalism as a signal that they are tolerated, so they persist or worsen. In software development, the analogy is that a team that regularly experiences disrepair — such as sporadic outages, broken builds, and poor code — comes to see them as normal; not only does the team not improve the situation, they are not alarmed if it deteriorates. The result is crufty (messy and poorly written) code that people are afraid to touch, builds that increasingly require manual intervention, and thousands of known defects. Getting out of this bad situation is sometimes impossible without a full rewrite.

The Broken Windows theory has a positive side, too: maintaining the environment in a good state will prevent escalation, and thereby prevent nasty surprises. Since Agile teams believe the theory, they bolster their implementation of continuous quality with several practices meant to prevent deterioration:

+ "All hands on deck" or "swarming" in times of crisis: everyone (not just an expert) comes together to solve the problem and prevent recurrence.

+ "The Boy Scout Rule": if you work on some part of the product, leave that area a bit cleaner than you found it.

✦ Test and demo an iteration's code in environments that max-imally resemble the production environment.

✦ Hold special retrospectives to learn lessons from outages and firefighting, as well as from certain features that turned out to be very hard to build.

And as if this discipline weren't enough, Agile throws another principle into the mix: reliability. What the team does in a time-box should not jeopardize or compromise their ability to work properly in a later time-box. When they execute tasks from their backlog, their actions should not reduce the intrinsic quality of their product. The popular way to think of this is to work "cleanly." For instance, after my dentist finishes work on my filling, her team cleans up the instruments she used and readies the room for the next patient. This cleanup is a normal part of the work.

The default Agile prioritization of project constraints is to put time first (choose when you'll release the product) and then quality (do your best work during that time-box). This ordering is appropri-ate if users want your product early, and if they want it to work well; as needed, you can negotiate scope and costs.

In many organizations, however, choosing quality over scope is a courageous decision. Teams are expected to turn out product con-tent (in the form of capability or behavior). Since content is what the users need and request, it becomes the measure of success. That makes scope front-of-mind for managers and teams alike. Unfortu-nately, quality is something that users notice only after receiving the product, and then it's mostly the absence of quality that frustrates the users and hurts the team. Put another way, if you're developing a product, lack of scope is something you pay for *now*, while lack of quality is something you pay for *later*. Quality has to do with delight-ing your users; scope has to do with satisfying them by getting the nominal job done. If you truly value product quality, you may have to take a strong stand for it, and that takes courage.

> "Answering questions about quality vs. scope is difficult for us, because they force us to look inwards and define ourselves."
>
> *– Jay, product owner at an investment firm*

Safety

You cross the street at the lights. You shun food that smells bad. You wear goggles, gloves, or special clothing when doing something dangerous. You dress up when it's cold and you drink a lot of liquids when it's hot. In everyday life, you take safety measures, but you're never 100% safe. How safe are you when working?

> In utilities and trades, safety comes first. A few days before I wrote this, someone banged loudly and repeatedly on my front door. It was a representative of the gas utility, wearing a hard hat and full workman's gear, come to give an estimate about moving a pipe (in other words, he wasn't supposed to do any work on the house that day). I asked him, "Why didn't you just ring the doorbell?" He answered, "If there's any kind of leak, the electric current from the doorbell might cause an explosion. We don't take risks; our procedure is to knock on the door."

Agile practitioners expect their organizational environment to be safe, which is a matter of culture and leadership. Such an environment enables them to:

+ Give feedback and discuss sensitive matters without fear of reprisal. (That is why retrospectives without safety are a waste of time.)

+ Know their boundaries and exercise their autonomy within those boundaries without being shot down.

✦ Understand the organization's values and act on them without hesitation.

✦ Retain their physical and psychological health (for instance, by maintaining a sustainable pace).

✦ Enjoy respectful, sensible, and consistent treatment from everyone.

Within a safe environment, Agile teams like to *work safely*. To that end, they decompose large work into small tasks, each of which is small, safe, and feedback-rich: it ends quickly, there's quick and useful feedback at the end, and if that feedback is negative, they can backtrack or "undo" that task's work. They rely on colleagues, tools, and processes to provide the feedback. They never have to be in the dark. They never take big gambles without frequent opportunities to validate their direction and, if necessary, change their minds.

I wrote *The Human Side of Agile* in Microsoft Word, and once the text had gone through reviews and edits, it was time to design and lay out the print edition. I wanted the experience with my designer to be collaborative, stepwise, and *safe*. So initially, she laid out two pages and asked for my opinion. Then she laid out a page that had a story (like this one); it didn't feel right to me, so we iterated once more. Then she designed chapter headings, asked for my feedback, and so on. This was safe for me, because I got an early feel for her competence and the quality of the result. The designer was able to experiment safely, rather than base a single design pass on guesses, her previous work, and the confining framework of a fixed-price contract.

Safety minimizes unpleasant surprises, whether personal or organizational, so it confers a clear benefit of reliability. And when we employ humans to do work, safety has a secondary benefit: it takes their fear away. All knowledge workers experience fears; here are a few examples from software development, which is rife with fear:

- ✦ Developers: writing a feature correctly under time pressure; making a code change without knowing what they broke elsewhere

- ✦ Testers: having killer defects escape to production; checking functionality without knowing for certain how the system should behave

- ✦ Product managers: forgoing important and seemingly simple features because of crazy (but realistic) estimates; drawing product roadmaps that might not hold up

- ✦ Managers: having to commit to an improbable timeline; watching a key team member depart when the going is already tough

- ✦ Project managers: not accounting for tasks on the critical path; being criticized for not keeping control of "their" project

When their fear is gone, or reduced to tolerable levels, people feel confident to keep moving and finish the work. Unfortunately, many popular ways to reduce fear also reduce safety. In the above examples, these ways include indifference, ignoring others' needs, micromanagement, pulling rank, and overtime. All of these are human responses, not a dictation of any particular process, so they may not be entirely avoidable. The Agile set of values, beliefs, and principles creates an environment that increases safety, and thereby likely reduces fear. On a personal level, if you work in such an environment, you can expect the following:

- ✦ Because the whole team is playing in the same game, there's no need to worry about others' reactions. Communicate respectfully and collaborate on achieving your joint purpose. Even if you drop the ball, others have your back. Whatever happens, it's not about you personally, it's about the team.

✦ Whatever your role, you'll deliver when you can, at your capacity, based on agreements. Besides, you alone are *not* singularly responsible for delivery, even if you're the manager.

✦ There is always a next time. If your actions are not accomplishing intended results, a reflection opportunity is just around the corner, and you'll be able to do better next time.

Visibility

Jose, the project manager, was nervous. The program manager had asked him for a detailed progress report, and Jose wasn't sure how to translate the team's release and iteration plans to the percent-complete, tracking-to-plan type of report that Dennis, the program manager, was used to. "Why don't you invite Dennis to the team's space and show him our boards?" I asked Jose. "Explain how you and the team plan, track work, and deal with impediments and risks."

The next day Jose was beaming. "It only took 10 minutes," he said, "for Dennis to understand our artifacts. He told me to forget the report, he'll just come in whenever he needs data and look at the whiteboards."

Every system for managing a team's work needs information about progress, and Agile is no different. A distinguishing factor of Agile, however, is its insistence on making such information *visible* to every team member. Practitioners aren't keen on information that's merely *available*, tucked away in a document graveyard or electronic system: out of sight, out of mind. What's *in* sight, on the other hand, draws attention, sparks conversations, and influences behavior. Since there is only so much room on a team's walls — or on their intranet's homepage — Agile teams choose carefully what information they make visible, which falls into two categories.

The first and obvious category includes information about the work. Basic information helps coordinate work among the members of a self-organizing team, and includes the plan for the release/ iteration and the state of each item. There are several popular means to express progress, and every team, program, and organization decides what's worth tracking and what's not. Since the main focus is on completing work, many teams arrange their information about work items visually, so they can easily see delays and bottlenecks. They might add elements to represent impediments or breakage, such as a traffic light for showing build status.

The other category of information supports teamwork. Typical artifacts include the one-page project charter, to always remind the team of the big picture and their project's justification, and team agreements, which reinforce desired behavior.[4] I've coached teams who put up additional information to support their dynamics: an absence chart, a skills matrix, a who's-paired-with-whom-this-week matrix, reminders in large fonts, action items from retrospectives, and so on.

Having a visible indicator of finished work is a great catalyst of teamwork. Many teams advertise the number of completed work items by putting a graph on the wall. One team I coached got a jar and would just throw the crumpled sticky notes indicating finished items into it. And, as shown in the picture, whenever the notes reached a certain level, the team would celebrate that with a fun, low-cost event.

Moving the work along and supporting teamwork are enough to justify visibility mechanisms. Some teams use them for a third purpose: earning the trust of managers and stakeholders. Trust is built gradually, and one side has to go first; by being transparent about their work and making their progress public knowledge, a team sends the message that *they* won't be the cause of unpleasant surprises. Over time, management comes to trust the team to deliver reliably. This helps management do their own planning and encourages them to allow the team greater autonomy — which further increases their reliability.

Cost of Change

Applying new learning, acting on feedback, and being responsive are three keys to Agility, all of which result in changes to the team's product. To apply them while remaining productive, the cost of those changes must remain as low as possible throughout the product's natural growth. We've seen some of the planning mechanisms that help control a product's cost of change: iterations, semiautonomous teams of business and technology people, prioritization and "You Aren't Gonna Need It" (YAGNI), deferring decisions, and splitting items. When acting on a particular work item, additional mechanisms are available.

Comprehensive definition of "Done." Have a standard of completion (definition of "Done") that means you can truly put items to bed and move on. Beyond acceptance by the product owner and no obvious defects, a useful standard sets expectations for the quality, cleanliness, and documentation of the item's construction. Of course, you actually have to work to that standard; a popular counterexample in software development is leaving "to-do" comments in the code. A high standard of completion might seem to cost a bit after you're apparently done with the item, but it prevents the higher costs of relearning and dealing with surprises. It allows you to assume, the next time you work on a related area, that the product is sound, nothing needs to be fixed before you start, and no surprises will come your way.

Simplicity. Agile practitioners sometimes confuse a high standard of completion with a comprehensive solution. An Agile principle that helps clear the confusion is *simplicity*. A simple solution goes to the heart of the problem and has no extra bits that might apply to a future problem that isn't being solved yet. A simple deliverable is compact and succinct, and addresses only what's needed; future changes (to the problem or the solution) will have less to touch.

For example, consider a co-located team just starting with Agile: they need some means to capture their work items and plans. If they choose a software tool, they'll need to configure it to match their process, and they must continue to do so anytime they modify it. Early in a team's life cycle, that happens a lot; in fact, some tools' cost of configuration change discourages teams from making certain process adaptations. Alternatively, the team might choose a simpler solution — sticky notes, whiteboard, and markers — which takes little configuration and is easy to alter. Once their process stabilizes and their backlog grows, a one-time cost of switching to a software tool might be worth paying.

Reduced inertia. Classical physics has taught us that an object's inertia — the difficulty of changing its speed and direction — grows with its mass. Similarly, product development organizations experience greater inertia when they act on large commitments and make elaborate plans. Worse, once they've started a large change initiative, it must run its course. To keep the cost of change low, evaluate every decision: Will it create or increase inertia? If so, consider other options. A good heuristic for avoiding inertia is to work on small items and take small steps.

A painful example I see all the time is companies confidently rewriting a major framework ("We're building infrastructure for the future") or revamping their application's user interface ("This time we'll get it right!"). They commit many people to implement it over many months. Once started, these folks can make few changes cheaply, and sunk costs deter managers from making strategic changes. Even a decision to stop the initiative is costly, since any integrated code must be tested.

If you regularly ship your product when iterations end, that will keep the cost of change under control. That said, even if you're not planning to ship at the end of the *current* iteration, act as if you will. Doing so will reduce the amount of work left hanging at the end of the time-box, and will reinforce the behaviors mentioned above: do clean, simple, and small work.

Specializing generalists (also known as "T-Shaped People"). A sometimes-hidden factor of the cost of change is *who* makes it: Do they know how to make the change, and can they get to it in a timely manner? Teams should have a suitable mix of skills and abilities, although these are rarely distributed equally. This often creates a preference in the team to assign work to specialists. However, not all work requires specialists; generalists — reasonably competent and knowledgeable team members — may perform such work to acceptable standards. If most of a team's work can be done by *specializing generalists*,[5] and if the members can become such contributors, they can reduce the cost of delay and consequently the cost of change.

Seeing Agile iterations merely as a planning and coordination mechanism is risky. There's a lot to be said for how a team approaches execution: finishing without delay and making their progress visible, keeping quality high and the cost of change low, and staying safe. Real-world experience has shown that without Agile-minded execution, a team won't remain Agile for long. So be sure to follow these principles when designing your process.

Every chapter in this book describes the Agile approach independently of its domain of application — every chapter, that is, except for the next one. Since the mid-'90s, the Agile mind-set has been embraced in various disciplines, yet none more so than in software development. If that is your work, read the next chapter for additional guidance on doing that work. Otherwise, skip that chapter and go on to chapter 8.

Chapter 7
Doing the Work, Part II
When It's Software Development

As we saw in chapter 1, the set of Agile principles is typically a good fit for work situations where the Agile values and beliefs apply. One such area is technology development. Agile methods are most widely used there, with the highest number of practitioners being in software development, where Agile thinking was born and where most of its thought leaders still come from.

The activities of software development make various processes and practices possible that are irrelevant to the development of tangible products, such as whiteboard markers or exercise treadmills.

Because software is all digital — it boils down to characters in files — it is infinitely malleable. If we don't like a feature's implementation, we can use a computer to change it. We don't have to limit ourselves to having humans test our software; we can write automated tests, which are software code in their own right. Changes to deployed software products (such as upgrades and fixes) may be much cheaper than changes to deployed physical goods.

Those same characteristics also make the development of software far more challenging than that of other products. Some of the top reasons for that are:

Configurability. Customer A wants some feature enabled, but Customer B doesn't? It can take five minutes to introduce a configuration parameter to the software. Unfortunately, those five minutes result in a hidden, and often nasty, increase to the cost of change.

> Long ago, I joined a company that sold wealth management software to five large banks. The software platform already had more than 1,000 configuration parameters and required extensive custom adaptations. Changing anything in the platform would result in changes to those customizations and require heavy testing. Requests for platform enhancements had to go through long review cycles before being approved.

Statefulness. You can start using software, go away for a while, and later pick up where you left off: the software will remember your "state." With modern computing power, that state can be quite detailed. The testing of functionality — a key feedback loop in software development — becomes very expensive when the tests also need to worry about many possible starting points.

Opaque construction. If you used inappropriate or poor-quality elements to build a chair or a car, the results would quickly show. In software, functionally correct but poorly constructed elements can get the nominal job done, only to spring high maintenance costs on you when you're least prepared for them. In fact, as any programmer knows all too well, programs can be written to perform pretty much any kind of service; the hard part is doing that within desirable business criteria such as schedule, cost, quality, and maintainability. The opacity of construction makes managers mistake prototypes for deployment-grade products, hire unqualified personnel, and struggle to gauge progress.

Complexity. Even the smallest building blocks of software are complex. What's worse, those building blocks depend intricately on one another, magnifying the impact of small errors. It is mentally taxing to read code and accurately follow its logic and state.

These aspects of software development have led many people to believe that it's a messy activity. Traditional remedies include detailed documentation, tools and frameworks, code reviews, specializations, and supervisory roles (such as technical lead, development manager, and QA manager). Agile practitioners don't think that software development is necessarily messy; rather, they believe they can prevent much of the mess by keeping the complexity of software in check.

Agile software development practitioners apply everything you've encountered in the book thus far (so make sure to read all the preceding chapters first). When it comes to *doing the work*, however, the guidance of the previous chapter is not enough, given the possibilities and challenges of their profession. This chapter lays out what technical Agility means in software development.

[*Note:* The activities in software development don't all benefit from Agility the same way. Key Agile concepts, such as feedback, learning, and adaptability, are very useful to the parts usually associated with development teams: specification, design, coding, and testing. The later activities — verification, packaging, and deployment — benefit more from manufacturing-minded values such as efficiency and repeatability, and are not discussed in this book.]

Design

As we've seen, Agile reframes the concept of "requirements," dividing them into problems/needs you have now, ones you'll have later, and ones that you *might* have later. The mind-set guides you to solve *just* the problems of now, without creating a solution so incompatible with likely futures that it would be soon thrown out. You repeat this exercise, looking in every cycle at any "later problem" that has materialized as a true "now problem." In other words, an Agile-developed solution emerges and evolves. You rely on feedback loops and learning opportunities to inform this evolution, which is both *incremental* (more pieces get added) and *iterative* (some pieces get changed).

The implication in software is that the traditional "big design up front" approach (BDUF, in Agilese) is a questionable practice. BDUF is the thing to do when you value efficiency across the development life cycle and getting the result right the first time — that is, where you'd want to apply the Waterfall model — but if you value adaptability, design changes will be costly. Moreover, BDUF inhibits change; after all, if you've spent months producing a design document, and it's been reviewed and approved, how inclined would you be to change things around?

"One of our first projects after transitioning from Waterfall to Agile required the software to have a solid, scalable architecture. As the company still believed in individual stars over great teams, the product's architecture became the responsibility of a single senior person, considered the best developer in the company. He spent months creating a highly complex architecture without consulting other team members, and then developed the entire back-end of the product. All this time, other team members felt alienated and disconnected from the project.

> "The architecture proved to be severely flawed. Technical debt was rampant. The budget was blown, the developer ended up leaving the company, and many new team members had to work with his design. The project was delivered at 3x the initial budget, took 4x longer than expected, and cost the company one of its most important clients."
>
> *– Employee at a Web development agency*

Agile software developers value design a great deal, and they have a different approach than BDUF. Assuming which bits are likely to change frequently guides the timing and depth of their design activities. Collaboration with their customers, keeping the end in mind, and experience help firm up their assumptions. They typically design the stable and invariant aspects early — that's being both effective *and* efficient — and defer design decisions for high-change items to the last responsible moment. They opt for simplicity in their designs as well as in their tools, using the simplest modeling approaches that can support communication, feedback, and shared understanding.

> Applications need to deal with data. Most developers, through education and conditioning, believe that applications require databases and appropriately designed data schemas. That is true...but only sometimes. I've worked with several teams where an early introduction of a database would have been the equivalent of wearing a straitjacket. Instead, we stored data in flat text files. This design choice eliminated the drag on our progress on riskier or more valuable parts of the software, such as usability. Once most of the product's discovery was over — which took two years in one of those cases — we replaced the flat files with a suitable database.

As we've also seen, when it comes to the "incremental" part of evolution, each increment ought to be *solid*. For instance, if an increment adds a field to a form, the team adds proper handling of the new piece of data to all affected layers and components, *and* makes necessary low-level design changes so the addition doesn't leave a scar. Or, if the next increment adds complexity to some business logic, they also update all the pieces that depend on it or support it, including architecture. With each increment, the team keeps the design, construction, interfaces, behavior, and flow in lockstep: the result is releasable and in good working order. This is easier to do when increments are small and simple.

One manifestation of the "iterative" part of evolution is found in changes to existing functionality. If the decision is made (typically due to feedback) that some previously developed behavior needs to change, a work item will capture the information about the new change. The development team would treat it the same way as an increment: make it solid, simple, and sufficient, and then implement it in a sequence of small, safe steps. Read more on this in the "Small Steps" section of this chapter.

The other manifestation of "iterative" occurs when building upcoming increments, or getting ready for them, requires changes to the design and implementation, but *not to the functionality or purpose*, of some existing code. Making those changes is called *refactoring the code*. Unlike rewriting, refactoring is a transformation, such as renaming a variable, changing a function's arguments or location, or extracting duplicate fragments into shared code.

Since refactoring doesn't appear to add customer value, many customers and managers mistakenly see it as penalty for poor execution or bad decisions. Those do happen and do incur cost, but they are (hopefully) the exception. Instead, Agile teams rely on refactoring as an intentional practice. Wanting to get to "Done" without delay, they develop simple, sufficient, and safe code for their increments — the problems they're solving now. Once that code needs to grow, they'll refactor it to make room for whatever that growth happens to be. While refactoring is a technical practice, it supports business decisions; it is analogous to paying back the principal and interest on money you borrowed in order to seize opportunities. In this analogy, a team that writes good, clean code, at a level of complexity that's good enough for now but not for the future, is said to be taking on "*technical debt.*" By contrast, a team that does shoddy, hasty, or throwaway work is creating cruft, and will pay a higher penalty for it later.

Back in 2000, my team was developing a new Java-based Web application. When we wanted to make the server's port configurable, one of my colleagues wrote the method `savePort()` and chose a simple storage mechanism: a Properties file. A few days later, someone made the server's address configurable; through the magic of copy and paste the almost-identical method `saveAddress()` was born. A third person then became the code's "owner" and added more parameters over time. A few months later, he went on vacation and I was asked to help. I discovered that whenever he needed to add a parameter, he just added to that Java class a copy of the save method, merely changing its name and the name of the parameter. That class already had more than 300 lines of code, duplicated across almost 20 methods, just for saving parameters. Before continuing, I removed the duplication and reduced the code to a couple of methods taking up about 30 lines.

The first guy's solution was just what Agile practitioners would do: simple, legible, sufficient. The next guy went the simple way — copy and paste — and got the code working, but didn't clean up after himself. The next developer, who became the so-called owner, got the cruft snowball rolling. His manner of duplicating code wasn't even efficient, because it cost us in testing. When I cleaned up the 20 cases of duplication, I paid the team's penalty. An Agile team, by contrast, would immediately get nervous when they found three copies of anything and would be anxious to remove the duplication.

Both the iterative and the incremental aspects of software evolution tend to be stumbling blocks for the new-to-Agile. In those teams, developers believe that they will have no time to clean up, improve the implementation, or upgrade the design of their code. Once they are done with a feature, they believe, it's on to the next one, and no touching that feature again because there's an expected velocity to maintain. Whether their belief is justified or not, their recourse as professionals — and as people who want to remain employed — is to do BDUF. However, iterations rarely offer enough time for meaningful BDUF. What happens next is quite predictable. People start complaining about Agile. They clamor for longer iterations. They do BDUF anyway, miss iteration commitments, and habitually roll unfinished work into subsequent iterations. This way, they turn iterations from a change-enabling mechanism to an overhead. Your choice is simple: if you value change and intend to allow it, you must allow it in the code as well. If no substantial change is forthcoming and the team will not go back to this code after finishing it, do more upfront design.

Testing

My clients often ask me: "What's the best tool for Agile testing?"

Pause here. Take a few seconds to think about it. What do *you* think is the best tool for Agile testing?

Most testers (and test managers) are surprised by my answer, which isn't Selenium, Fitnesse, QTP, Ruby, or some other software or scripting language. My answer is: it's between your ears.

The best tool for Agile testing is a critical mind.

On the next page is a picture of my old phone on the morning after Daylight Savings Time kicked in in North America in 2011. Look at it for a few seconds. Really look at it and think about what you're observing in it.

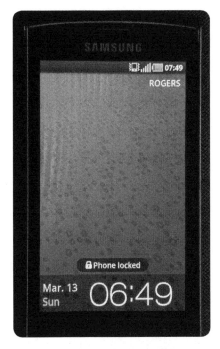

What did you notice?

If you have an eye for detail and differences, chances are you noticed that the big clock on the bottom says 06:49, whereas the status line on top shows the correct time, 07:49.

If you're a tester, you probably think at this point: Can I reproduce this problem? How did we miss that?

If you're an *Agile tester*, you'll probably ask an additional question: Why is the phone showing *two clocks*?

With this question, you've moved from problem thinking to critical thinking. You're critiquing the phone's design: How come the phone's user has to look at two clocks, instead of one? Wouldn't one do just fine? Is this creating a problem or perhaps an opportunity? What else could be going on with the phone's time-keeping or its lock screen?

This kind of testing involves no test cases, steps-to-reproduce, fancy tool, requirements document, traceability matrix, or specification. Just a human mind engaging with a product and asking... *Why? How come? What else? What if...?*

Testing a product, you still look for expected problems, of course. Some of its areas still deserve comprehensive checking and detailed analysis. With Agile testing, you also frequently apply your critical thinking skills to boost extrinsic quality.

Too often, testers are locked into the reactive mode of checking the product for conformance to someone else's requirements, of giving a compliance stamp. That's the "test plan" thinking pattern.

The best Agile testers I know go beyond verification and help make products great by critiquing the thinking that went into them. They do so throughout the life cycle: in deciding what to work on, in planning the work, in executing it, and finally in exploring the evolving product. This way, they truly collaborate in the *development* of software, as opposed to its manufacture.

Sapient testing (i.e., relying on skilled people) is on one end of the testing spectrum. On the opposite end are automated tests: pieces of code that check other code, and complain if expectations are not met. Such tests apply no critical thinking whatsoever: they capture previous thinking and agreement about behavior. Their most obvious benefit is in detecting breakage ("regression"), which is particularly useful feedback if the tests are fast; they can help teams prevent unintended quality degradation. Even though writing such tests comes at a cost, the cost of well-written, relevant, behavior-focused tests is often lower than the cost of investigating and fixing breakage. Their other benefits are covered in the next section.

Agile developers confer the same "first-class citizen" status to their automated tests as to their production code. They keep them in the same repository and maintain them as necessary. Tests have the following properties:

+ **Fast**. If a test suite (a collection of tests) is slow, that's not just slow feedback. The team will simply not use it as much, which is almost as bad as no feedback.

+ **Minimal liability**. The iterative and incremental nature of Agile work shouldn't cause expensive reworking of tests. This typically requires that the tests inspect behavior, not implementation.

+ **Executable documentation**. Since the tests inspect behavior, it's preferable to write them in a way that demonstrates the usage of that behavior. A team member should be able to understand the behavior's context, inputs, and outputs merely from browsing the test. Think of the tests as a communication medium; it increases shared understanding, and reduces the waste involved in maintaining parallel explanations in English.

✦ **Collectively owned.** The tests belong to the team, not to select members.

Small Steps

In planning their next iteration, Agile teams intend to address the next few items that would make the greatest difference. A typical work item in their plan is likely to be some functionality, behavior, or aspect of the software, and to involve small increments and changes to existing code.

Even though those items are small — each one typically needing only a few days of work — many development teams dive into their implementation with a non-Agile mind-set. How? Their education, experience, and habits guide them to first design, then code, and finally test each item. But exactly like at higher levels of planning and execution, this sequential, functional approach assumes certainty and knowledge that may be unjustified. And when that's the case, the typical results of working in this sequential manner are incomplete deliverables, missed expectations, and planning overhead.

I often see this dynamic play out when a team needs to change the design (but not behavior) of an active, integrated component. The common approach to this is to code and test the new design in isolation, integrate it, toss the old design, and fix any breakage. The developers mean to be efficient, but their approach tends to be so unsafe that the task soon turns into a bottomless pit. In a recent example, a developer confidently estimated a redesign task at five days. Twelve days and several uncomfortable status checks later, he thought he was done (but he wasn't sure...).

Approaching a work item with the Agile mind-set would mean completing it as a series of micro-items. Using similar ideas as they would for splitting (see chapter 3), practitioners look for small pieces of the item that would move it closer to a shippable state through learning, feedback, adaptation, or simplicity. Since programmers implement behaviors and functionality in their code, they keep asking:

"What's the next micro-behavior?"

(Or, "What's the next micro-functionality?")

For instance, if my work item is to calculate the sales tax on a shopping cart's total, I could start coding the calculation for single-tax cases (such as the European VAT) and later deal with double-tax cases (such as provincial and federal in some parts of Canada). I could approach the first case, the single tax, using this sequence of micro-behaviors:

1. Calculate the tax when the cart has no taxable items.

2. Calculate the tax when the cart has one taxable item.

3. Calculate the tax when the cart has several taxable items.

4. Deal with exceptions, such as minimal threshold for taxation.

Each micro-behavior doesn't take much time and is fairly easy to get right: I can come up with a couple of examples of inputs (the items in the cart) and expected results (the tax payable on those items). Testing my work in progress using these examples keeps me safe — I'm not likely to inadvertently cause grave damage. I get quick feedback about the quality of my design. I can even pause almost anytime without leaving my code looking like a construction zone. Along the way, my work is even releasable, albeit in a limited context.

Notice how, in each step, I consider the next micro-behavior, and prove the correctness of my implementation? That is why you're more likely to hear Agile developers phrase the question a bit differently:

"What's the next test?"

Agile developers create software test-by-test. The alternative — to preconceive the components, algorithms, connections, objects, and other moving parts before constructing them — is hard to get right. The devil's in the details, which tend to be numerous and everywhere. Just like at the macro level, the Agile approach at the micro level isn't meant to optimize the time-to-solution but to optimize the chance of getting it right. If you're able to automate fast tests along the way, they will help you avoid nasty surprises — and resolve any surprises quickly and safely — so your progress will be reliable.

A well-known but deeply misunderstood technique that implements this approach, along with several Agile principles and values, is test-driven development (TDD). Each TDD cycle starts with identifying the next micro-behavior and proceeds with three steps. In the first ("Red"), developers write a small test that demonstrates the micro-behavior and fails because it's not implemented yet. In the second step ("Green"), they build or change just enough code to make the new test pass, all the while ensuring that every test still passes. In the third step ("Refactor"), they adapt the design to support the new behavior seamlessly.

The TDD cycle is formulated to keep developers safe (by only designing for known, proven usage), to keep their results simple but not crufty, and to allow feedback and learning. Repeated application of the cycle to additional micro-behaviors guarantees getting to "Done" and delivering value. While the tests created along the way are certainly useful for catching regressions, TDD is a perfect example of software development as an adaptive learning activity, as opposed to a predictable one that can be optimized for efficiency. Some teams also perform TDD cycles inside of larger cycles known as acceptance test-driven development (ATDD). While this practice also results in useful tests, it has bigger aims: a quick feedback loop between business and technology, beginning with the end in mind, and shared understanding through effective communication.

TDD exemplifies another Agile pillar we met in chapter 4: create processes that respect the workers' humanity. Developers can be easily convinced to write automated tests, but they'll default to "test-after": once they've written and thoroughly understood a piece of code, they'll write tests to cover it. One common pitfall is their motivation and available time to do so, after presumably being done coding. Another pitfall is that such tests don't age well. They are too closely tied to the implementation, which on an Agile project changes through iterative and incremental work. Soon enough, the tests stop compiling or passing. By writing their tests *before* the code, developers are not tempted to rely on the implementation, so they inevitably focus on the requirement or behavior.

> Within several months of adjusting my work habits to test-first, I wasn't just producing simpler and more concise code; I started believing that test-after was too risky for my own good. If I wrote code without having a test first, I would get worried.

Reliable Progress

An Agile team delivers value early and frequently. To do so, they proceed by completing small items and continuously validating their work; working on small pieces gives them greater control. Since they prefer effectiveness to efficiency, they don't try to progress *predictably*; rather they proceed *reliably*, which also makes their estimates meaningful. A useful strategy for making reliable progress is to minimize nasty surprises. The usual sources of such surprises in programming are unexpected code behaviors, integration of code, multitasking, and last-minute heroics. Let's examine the Agile approach to each one.

Unexpected code behaviors. Programming is such cognitively demanding work that keeping accurate track of all code dependencies, expectations, and consequences is impossible. Modern platforms, languages, design methods, and tools only partially control the chaos.

Many developers avoid touching code — other people's code, or their own from a few months back — because they fear the consequences. They can take some of the fear away by collaborating with colleagues, as well as by "buying insurance" on their software in the form of good test coverage. With tests, they can prove that they are building code right and that it stays that way. Automated low-level tests reduce the highest unpredictable expense of software change: fixing defects.

Agile software development teams typically need to balance sapient testing with automated testing. Each has distinct benefits and costs, and, like everything else in Agile, context is everything. A simple Agile mantra, which helps build good habits, is "No moving without a test!"

> Developers often interpret this mantra as "No moving without *an automated* test," which can limit their options. One team was working on a greenfield project, and within a few months the largest class in their Java codebase had 1,300 lines of complex code and no automated tests. I collaborated with one of the developers to clean it up some. We had no time to write useful automated tests, but we realized that a certain manual test case, which would take only three minutes to run, would let us trust our changes. Over that day and the next, we extracted 25% of the class into smaller, coherent pieces, and to stay safe, we ran that manual test cycle at least 20 times. While far from pristine, the result was good enough for the team to move confidently forward.

Integration. The second common reason of unreliable progress is the integration of code from two or more programmers. If each one finishes his or her "own part," putting the parts together is akin to digging a tunnel by starting at both ends: you plan to meet in the middle, but you may be off by quite a bit. To reduce this risk, developers work on small items and constantly communicate with each other — both in plain language and in code — to make sure that they connect properly (and that the integrated behavior is correct).

A common interpretation of the practice of "Continuous Integration" is to have a frequent build of the code that the team checked in to the shared repository during the day. This is a good feedback loop, but it's not nearly as useful as having the day's collection of small increments and changes actually be integrated *with each other* and proven to work *together*. Developers seem to take a bit longer to produce code this way, but it's in better shape. In particular, they prevent much of the headache of discovering and fixing integration errors at the end. Following the same logic, Agile teams prefer to minimize code branching.

Multitasking. The third common source of unreliable progress is multitasking. Thinking that it increases efficiency — even proudly putting their ability to multitask on their resumes — developers are prone to start working on some area and, along the way, start doing something else. Now they have two complex activities on the go; they are likely to finish both of them later, have trouble verifying the correctness of each one, and do less than excellent work on them. (It will also exhaust them.) The safer, more reliable way is to sequence their activities: finish whatever they start before doing the next thing.

Considering the high cost of reading code, programmers are wont to engage in a specific form of multitasking known as "While I'm There." For example, a few minutes into fixing a defect, a programmer is noticing an opportunity to refactor some related code — and decides to start refactoring while the bug fix is in progress, as opposed to fixing first and refactoring second. "While I'm There" is not only a pitfall due to multitasking; it's also a dangerous misinteptation of "the Boy Scout Rule," which we encountered in the previous chapter as a practice to control cruft.

Heroics. Finally, we have "crunch-time development," "Hail Mary passes," and other last-minute heroics. Every developer carries the battle scars of late nights spent finishing features. In those eleventh-hour efforts, fueled by caffeine and pizza, they mostly "dump code," writing it fast and furiously, just hoping to get it working before the deadline. Some teams, working in organizations that don't yet understand the Agile mind-set, experience this pressure every two weeks: when their sprint review comes up. While their heroics might seem to help them make good on their commitments for a few iterations, the fast buildup of cruft makes progress on later iterations unsafe, unreliable, and expensive. (Most don't have time to invoke the improvement principle, either — they don't clean up their act, so trouble is inevitable.) Doing quick and dirty work because of time pressure is only acceptable if the team takes time after the deadline to undo the cruft — and takes time to learn how to avoid a rerun of this situation.

Code Is for People

In every organization, one of the greatest assets is its people. Another great asset is the organization's products, since they bring in revenue. If those are software products whose upkeep or upgrading is expensive, they are also a liability. The common term for the code that runs them is "legacy code."

There is no standard definition for legacy code. A popular definition is "code without automated tests."[1] To others, legacy code is messy, hard to understand, and dangerous to touch. Some developers define legacy code as code someone else wrote (who, by inference, wasn't a great programmer). Since legacy code is assumed to work properly, it's not the user's problem; it's the builder's problem, and indeed, all the definitions refer to the shape the code is in, and to the team's cost of living with it. Most developers I know appreciate the business value derived from legacy code but take the same dim view of it as of other nuisances in life, like traffic jams and lines in stores.

No developer sets out to do shoddy work or create messes for other people. Legacy code gets to be the way it is one step at a time, with two obvious forces at play. One is schedule pressure, which doesn't leave developers enough time to do proper work. The other is the opacity of software, which makes it easy to ignore the quality of its construction once the thing seems to work. Yet these two forces don't make up the complete story. To this day, many developers and their managers operate with a set of beliefs that has them create legacy code unawares:

+ "Once we write something, we don't expect to come back to it much (other than to make a few small fixes)." This belief stems from the concept of working from vetted requirements; they are assumed to be valuable and correct, and remain this way for years.

+ "Whoever writes a piece becomes its owner (and will know where and how to fix problems)."

+ "The cost of making requirement changes (including fixing mistakes) grows exponentially the later in the life cycle you make them." This belief — known as the cost of change curve[2] — causes people to overplan and create too many unused or overcomplicated product parts.

+ "Other people will deal with the consequences of our actions." For instance, QA will find our bugs, sustaining engineering will fix them, and new developers will figure their way around by reading our documentation.

+ "With seniority and experience, a developer will write better code faster." Therefore, assigning work to task experts increases efficiency and reduces defects.

These beliefs are congruent with Waterfall thinking of minimizing time and expense. But if you're after the top Agile values — value delivery and responsiveness of *a team* — then optimizing any individual's coding is not a useful way to achieve them. Instead, the real driver is the team's ability to quickly upgrade, change, or fix code. To make that happen, developers must be able to read and understand it quickly. This is a communication problem.

In other words, traditional development optimizes for writing code, while Agile optimizes for reading and changing it. Thus, an Agile software development belief is that *Code Is for People*. After all, computers will understand whatever we throw at them, whether humans struggle to understand it or not. In support of this belief, Agile developers incorporate the following principles into their mind-set:

Write intent-revealing code. Reading a piece of code (and its tests, which are also code), a programmer who knows the context should easily follow the logic and the writer's thought process with minimal reliance on comments in English.

Write simple code. Don't make it more complex or generic than necessary. For instance, it shouldn't be optimized for speed of execution if the need for that hasn't been established.

Make it easy to come back to the code. Put things in obvious places, name them properly, be consistent, use standard constructs and patterns, remove dead code, and avoid "gotchas" (or explain them clearly).

Make tests the single source of truth (even if you may have misunderstood the truth). Use automated tests to document software behavior. The tests can be considered executable specifications.

Collaborate. Code is *for* people and *by* people. Reduce many of the risks of employing imperfect humans to write code (see chapter 4) by having them collaborate. The best-known mode for that is pair programming.[3]

Act as if no design is sacred. As software grows, new capabilities may outpace the design or be incompatible with it, no matter how awesome it was earlier. If that happens, change the design.

The pliable nature of software allows developers to collaborate with their business counterparts to evolve its design. They strive to make reliable progress while leaving open their options for change. They do so by decomposing work items into micro-behaviors and implementing them in clean, simple, and readable code. They automate tests to minimize angst, document behavior, and shorten feedback loops. Having good technical Agility allows software development teams to remain a true business asset, and to keep their products evolving viably over time.

We've looked at engaging people and teams to determine, plan, and do the work. We're not done yet, though. How can those people and teams work better? That is the subject of the next chapter.

SUPPLEMENTARY RESOURCE: Download "Technical Agility Self-Assessment" questionnaire from the book's companion website, **www.TheAgileMindsetBook.info**.

Chapter 8
Getting Better at Work

A key Agile principle is to always improve things. Your product, process, and teamwork will never reach perfection; you just keep making them better. Scrum calls this approach "inspect and adapt"; the other popular term is "continuous improvement." Previous chapters showed how an Agile team improves their product, while this chapter shows how they improve the process and teamwork by which they create that product.

What to Improve

Improvements to the team's process and work habits can have great effect on results. If people don't communicate well, create too many defects, build the wrong things, duplicate efforts, get stuck too often, or don't collaborate effectively — any reduction in these will improve the bottom line of delivered value. As well, it will directly support the manifestation of the Agile principles and thereby the achievement of the Agile values. Improving output metrics, however, can be risky business; every metric can be gamed, and sometimes the improvement can result in unpleasant side effects.

> "When some senior managers learned about the concept of 'velocity,' they mandated a 25% increase in velocity across all teams. The team that consistently delivered high quality happened to have the lowest velocity due to their conservative story point estimates, and was thus identified as a 'poor performing team.' Another team, which routinely deployed disappointing releases, had the highest velocity and was officially crowned the #1 team. In short order, all teams were increasing their story point estimates and velocity went through the roof. Soon, the Agile teams that were actually beginning to succeed could no longer use velocity for effective planning."
>
> *– John Hill, Agile Coach and Trainer*

Improvement efforts usually keep the mind-set unchanged while adapting its manifestation. It's less common, but still possible, that an improvement cycle would cause a team to revisit elements of the mind-set. For instance, they might value responsiveness, but discover that most changes are rare, insignificant, or undesirable, and that they can be both effective and efficient with a good deal of up-front planning. Or, if a team realizes that they never get enough useful feedback from their stakeholders, they might revise their process to fulfill a much-reduced expectation of external feedback.

Agile teams rely on various tactics to identify useful targets for improvement. The basic mode, which is how iteration retrospectives tend to run, uses collaborative methods to elicit and discuss members' observations and concerns. Teams might use metrics, measurements, or context-specific performance indicators. They may look to other disciplines, such as Lean thinking, for ideas such as mapping the value stream and looking for delays and bottlenecks. They might rely on industry resources and consultants for additional ideas.[1]

Early-stage teams can make great strides with basic reflective techniques. For instance, just by pondering "What worked well?" and "What could be improved?" in their first few iteration retrospectives, many teams have realized that they:

- ✦ Planned to complete more than they could handle, or

- ✦ Finished on time, but delivered little value, or

- ✦ Allowed too-frequent changes to the planned iteration work and thereby experienced rework, delays, and reduced team morale.

It took the software industry about a decade to realize that team-level improvements sometimes result in suboptimizing the value chain. For example, if Development pours out software at 10 times the rate Operations can move it to production, that's not too helpful. There is a similar impedance mismatch with sales and product development. Therefore, teams do well to consider the effect of their changes on the overall organization. Again, ideas from other disciplines come in handy, such as Lean and systems thinking.

As for productivity, the Agile mind-set considers the team's productivity to be markedly more important than individuals'. This is reflected in commonly used team-based units and measurements, such as velocity, story points, and work in progress limits. Individual ability and accomplishment are important only from the perspective of contributing to the team's ability and accomplishment — because in Agile, working product is the primary measure of progress.

In trying to embrace the Agile mind-set, many organizations have stopped short of elevating team productivity over individual productivity. While they appreciate teamwork, this principle is in direct conflict with entrenched policies and structures aimed at managing individual performance. The typical outcome of this resource management thinking is mediocre team performance and "super-star" (or "prima donna") behavior. If the members feel forced to choose between the good of their team and their own personal benefit or risk, their team will never thrive.

Thus, adaptation and improvement typically focus on how a team works together or how they get things done. Some examples from teams I've coached are:

+ Determining guidelines for making high-impact technical decisions

+ Simplifying their workflow

+ Reconfiguring their iteration board to show different work states

+ Trying various ways to determine who works on what when

+ Fleshing out a "Definition of Ready": the required characteristics of work items before the team can consume them

+ Experimenting with new practices

+ Negotiating "response level agreements" with their busy customer

+ Increasing their technical discipline

+ Petitioning to revoke a wasteful or cumbersome departmental policy

+ Organizing knowledge-sharing events to expand members' ability to contribute

"When we first started to use Scrum, we used an online tool to manage our board. I found myself having to remind the team frequently to update the board. In addition, our daily Scrum meeting had little benefit; team members mentioned ticket numbers they were working on, but some did not know exactly what those tickets were about.

"After a few months we decided to try a physical board instead. Everyone got a magnet with their picture, so they could indicate what they were working on. Creating this board forced us to reexamine our workflow, strengthen our definition of 'Done,' and add feedback loops for product acceptance and testing.

"The physical board made a difference from day one. Team members started to point at the work they were working on during the daily Scrum. They *wanted* to update the board and loved moving their magnets from task to task as they completed them. Our velocity increased. We started to see increased collaboration and some meaningful discussions about work on the go."

– Alon Sabi, CTO at Function Point Productivity Software

Whatever the change is, the team is going to live with it, so *they* decide what to change, and how. Therefore, deciding what to improve is a matter of team consensus. The team leader participates in making those decisions; being a servant leader, she doesn't impose her own thoughts on the team. Knowledgeable, helpful leaders may be heavily involved in improvement efforts; they just stop short of robbing the team of their autonomy and safety.

The same is true for the team's coach, if they have one. No matter how much a team may like me or believe me, they won't own an imposed change. Instead, I help teams improve by giving continuous feedback (and advice if asked) and facilitating timely reflection.

Just as a team avoids making commitments too large and too soon, so it is with their improvements. Rather than announce a binding change, the Agile mind-set guides them to experiment with it: try it over a defined period of time, collect data and feedback, then decide what to do. This approach is pragmatic, since even experts' suggestions may fail to yield improvements. Moreover, experimentation creates excitement and involvement, and therefore buy-in. It is an effective way to get the team to notice and care about process and how they work together.

Making Improvements

If you choose the Scrum framework, one of the required practices is the sprint (iteration) retrospective. When an iteration is over, everybody takes their hands off the keyboards to discuss the iteration's events in order to make the next one better. This practice relies on slack (see chapter 4) and team empowerment (see chapter 5) to support adaptation and better value delivery. Established as the end-marker of each iteration, which is typically only a couple of weeks long, it has teams consider improvements *frequently*. Even if they engage in no other "continuous improvement" activity, effective iteration retrospectives are among the top ways to adopt the Agile mind-set.

The continuous improvement principle is A Good Thing on several levels. Not having to design perfection at the outset, you can relax and simply focus on making valuable progress. By making improvements in small, regular doses, you can avoid becoming overwhelmed. Your team owns and shares responsibility for much of its improvement. You can also apply temporary fixes and countermeasures with the confidence that you'll replace them with proper measures soon enough.

This attractive — and critical — principle is not easy to apply in practice. Temporary fixes have a way of becoming permanent. For some people, the repetitive strain of small changes is worse than the experience of bigger, yet isolated, changes. In almost every team, some members drive change while others cling to old habits. And yet others just want to get some things right the first time and not have to worry about improving them.

One reason improvement efforts stall or sputter is their abstract nature. They require the considerable mental effort of shifting attention from the present and its pressures to the unknown future and how to make it better. Agile addresses this challenge by expecting teams to reflect and adapt *frequently*, but it sets no further expectations. Thus, teams have good control over the scope of improvement or change, and can make it practical and applicable for themselves.

A second reason is that everyone is simply too busy. There is always enough work to do and many good options for filling up available time. Opportunities for improvement are easily squeezed out and the urgent trumps the important. That is why the practice of holding iteration retrospectives is common to most Agile frameworks: if it's not optional, it becomes a habit, a regular part of doing business. It's also an application of the focus principle: even though you could consider process improvements any day, you'll probably do so more effectively by setting aside regular times for doing specifically that.

Retrospectives can be a habit, but by becoming *repetitive* and routine, they can lose their edge. When I conduct assessments of Agile teams whose performance has plateaued, I often find some teams that hold retrospectives whose results aren't actionable. Other teams believe there's little left to improve, and prefer to use the retrospective time for value-adding work. Only a few of those teams truly have little room for improvement when I meet them; even so, regularly coming back to the improvement principle helps them over the long run.

The biggest reason for stalled, lukewarm, or haphazard improvement is that the improvers are human. Change hurts, and until it stabilizes, mistakes might feel like failure.[2] Statistically, every team has several members who operate with a fixed mind-set as opposed to a growth one.[3] Improvement, to some, implies that there are deficiencies; looking for and pointing them out might be a risky proposition. In a business setting, team members may fear consequences from senior managers and stakeholders alike. It takes a respectful, supportive, and safe culture, as well as leadership, to shift people away from these positions and make continuous improvement an actionable principle.

SUPPLEMENTARY RESOURCE: Download "Ideas for Retrospective Topics" from the book's companion website, **www.TheAgileMindsetBook.info**.

The End-Goal

While the team's product may be improved as far as the business will invest in it, the team's performance — the results of applying their process and teamwork — has an upper limit. The limit is partly a function of individual members' potential. The organization in which they operate affects it further through its culture, bureaucracy, scale, and power structure.

Nevertheless, even when they've apparently streamlined operations and reached a high level of performance, their environment (context) might change. Such changes are usually as frequent as the business cadence, or even more so. When that happens, a team must first take care to remain effective — that is, to continue discovering and delivering good value. Only then may they adapt further, to become more efficient at doing so.

While adjustment to change is a normal part of an Agile team's life, the degree of required change varies wildly, depending on context. If they need to respond to a high degree of product, staffing, and technology changes, they should work on being dynamic; that takes openness, flexibility, and resilience.[4] If change is incremental, the technological landscape is fairly static, and staff turnover is low, then a team can be less dynamic, and can focus more on other attributes.

Either way, the ultimate goal of continuous improvement is something more significant than better value delivery and productivity. It is to become a *solid team*: a reliable team that the organization can rely on to execute on its mission within normal parameters.

As we saw in chapter 5, solid Agile teams come about with the support and cultivation of servant leaders. Such leaders maintain environments where such growth is possible: they are emotionally healthy and safe; personal and shared responsibility are the norm; and the whole set of principles of "Individuals and Interactions" is respected.

Welcoming change and responding to it are cornerstones of the Agile mind-set. Change may arise externally, for instance with shifting customer needs and business conditions. However, Agile teams also create change proactively on the inside, specifically by using feedback and learning so as to determine how to work better. Making regular improvements to their teamwork and process, they become a greater organizational asset over time. But how do they get to have the mind-set in the first place? Read on....

Chapter 9
Adopting the Mind-Set

We've seen how Agile approaches the various aspects of work: engaging people and teams, deciding what to do, planning it, doing it, and improving how it's done. But how do we adopt, embrace, and live the mind-set, as opposed to just "do" Agile and go through the motions?

Remember that the mind-set is contextual. You're not looking to *become* Agile exclusively. In a situation where your top values agree with the Agile ones, its principles might be a great fit. In another situation where different values matter, a non-Agile mind-set would be useful. Most readers of this book work in businesses where Agile-appropriate scenarios abound, affecting many people over long periods. This chapter explores how those people and businesses would adopt the mind-set.

It's a Whole System

Your starting point for identifying or determining your mind-set is the values: they are its highest level of abstraction. If you find the promise of Agile attractive, you must first and foremost consider its values: people before process, early and frequent value delivery, customer collaboration, and adaptation.

These values might look sensible and appealing, but they are certainly not an obvious choice for approaching work. If you trace the history of Agile, you'll know that the pioneers *discovered* them as the common denominator to their methods. In other words, the theory evolved from practice. Those early practitioners chose their methods because the absence of those values — software development managed as big-bang, change-averse projects staffed by interchangeable "resources" — seemed to hurt business. Agile has been one response to this situation; Lean is another. In a given situation, you might choose a different set of values and a different mind-set.

In the first 10 years of Agile, there was only small-scale, isolated experimentation with its principles. The following 10 years saw massive, worldwide experimentation that has solidified the mind-set. Even though it's still evolving — just like the world in which it exists — it's been fairly stable for a while; the principles in particular are a complete, field-tested, self-reinforcing system, as opposed to a hodgepodge of modern ideas.

You could decide to embrace the Agile value system and proceed to form your own beliefs and principles. While there is nothing wrong with this tactic, you would have few information sources, such as research and other people's experiences, to inform your choices. If you decide to go with "established Agile" — as explained in this book — you must truly embrace the full mind-set. That means abiding by the values, espousing the beliefs, and applying the principles. Some of them might have little relevance to your situation, but cherry-picking the ones to adopt tends to confuse people and yield mediocre results. For instance, allowing frequent change through iterative planning, while leaving most of quality assurance to the very end, often degrades intrinsic quality and protracts schedules.

In organizational settings, the person in the Agile customer role tends to be in a different organizational unit than the delivery team. **The next point cannot be emphasized enough:** Agile is not "just for the techies," or merely a way to expedite technology work. It is a paradigm in which both customer and developer collaborate toward an outcome that matters to both. Therefore, both parties need to agree to use Agile, to embrace the same mind-set, and to apply it in a way that works for both.

The engineering group at a telecom software company established Scrum in some of its teams in 2007. For years, their sprints, standups, demos, user stories, and retrospectives made little difference to the company's business. The product managers, who should have been acting as the teams' customers, would simply not work this way; everything was a must-have and they would plan and commit months out. Sprint planning didn't make sense to them, so engineering managers acted as product owners. Product Management had a strong Waterfall mind-set and they had no interest in Engineering's attempt at the Agile one. This went on for several years before senior management decided to get an Agile makeover.

When you embark on your Agile journey, start *something* with every principle at the same time, and gradually get better at applying all of them. This is especially important if you come to Agile from a contradicting mind-set. The alternative — adopting a few principles at a time, as if you had a backlog of them — might seem prudent, but it doesn't work because Agile is a complete system; many principles depend on others to make sense. Getting great at Agile, just like becoming great at long-distance running or at a new career or at parenting, involves a deep shift that a sequence of small steps cannot achieve adequately. You need to make a proper commitment: "Do it like you mean it."

It's a Transformation

Robert Dilts' "Logical Levels" model provides a conceptual, hierarchical explanation of how people go about life. Each of the levels in this model affects those below it, and supports the ones above it. The model is particularly useful in explaining the experience of change.[1] Here, we'll apply it to the change of mind-set.

The two upper levels, *identity* and *role*, are pivotal: they describe who you are, both in general and in specific contexts. They are about personality and

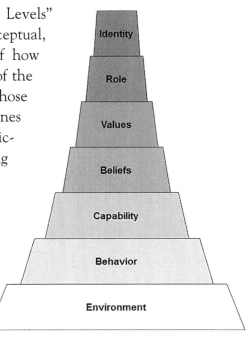

The Logical Levels of Change

how you place yourself in the world. For example, you might present yourself as "a project manager in telecom," or as "an Agile developer."

Mind-set lives in the next two levels, *values* and *beliefs*. For instance, as a project manager, you might place a premium on predictability and minimizing surprises. As an Agile developer, you might value technological progress. As long as your beliefs support your values, they could be quite different from those of someone else with the same role and values. For example, I know Agile developers who believe that every technology worker wants to make a difference; I also know others who believe that most professionals would take a solid paycheck over making a difference.

Mind-set, therefore, lives pretty high up in the Logical Levels hierarchy. If yours is already almost Agile, no problem. But what if it's not? Both in personality and in culture, values are often ingrained, and beliefs tend to be entrenched. Thus, it's disingenuous to proclaim, "From now on, I'm going to have this new mind-set. New things will be important to me and I will operate from a new set of convictions." The business counterpart of this statement is "We're going Agile, and expect to be done by year-end." *Telling* others to start being Agile is a nonstarter.

For individuals, embracing these values can mean a huge personal transformation. Consider, for instance, that mainstream Western classroom schooling doesn't sanction collaboration; students may learn together, but rarely produce together. Later as adults, when those students join the workforce, they are used to an environment that rewards individual output. School also teaches them to view feedback mostly as confirmation that they learned something correctly; it is rarely used as input to further learning and discovery.

So how does one kickstart a transformation? An easy way to get there — it's visible, tangible, and not too radical — is to "do Agile," which is to merely adopt practices commonly associated with it. When people first start doing Agile, they develop *capabilities*, exercise *behaviors*, and change their *environment*. For example, they meet daily to discuss progress and impediments, or learn to describe work items from the perspective of customer value, or paper their walls with sticky notes. In the Logical Levels model, these live in the bottom three rungs of the ladder.

According to the model, it is possible to effect a change at some level if it doesn't agree with the levels above it. For example, a team might well start writing user stories and having a daily standup meeting, while still valuing "getting it right the first time" and "minimizing resource expenditure." But before long, one of two things will happen: either the capability- and behavior-level changes will fizzle out and the situation will revert to the old status quo, or the higher levels will shift to align with the lower levels.

The first path is unfortunately the more common one. The higher levels — role, values, and beliefs — are in the driver seat. They will tolerate incongruent changes at the lower levels if there's a potentially useful outcome. But those levels also guide people when things go wrong, which they inevitably do. When the new behaviors create trouble or upset, or the new capabilities seem strange or risky, the higher levels will kick in to protect the person (or team, or organization). The mind-set will be tested in challenging situations! Therefore, if you start your path to change at the lower levels, first get good practice with the mind-set under regular, nonthreatening conditions.

In teams that are new to Agile, I often hear testers argue, "We like Agile, but we can't test properly without a spec." I observe developers do big design up front inside their iterations. I also see managers override team decisions. All these professionals usually act this way due to habit, training, and a fair level of anxiety: since they haven't become proficient at Agile yet, they feel irresponsible about ignoring their familiar practices. If there is a looming deadline, frequent firefighting, or close executive scrutiny, these are indeed acts of self-preservation. Individual contributors and managers have a better chance of adopting the Agile mind-set when the consequences of learning, struggling, or failing are not disastrous. They need to feel safe.

Getting on the second path — causing a shift in the higher levels toward the desired mind-set — requires openness to and awareness of the target. That target is a future self-image, and it must be appealing enough. Saying "I'm going to try writing user stories for a while and see if I like them" is not enough; you must understand their purpose, know what value that purpose serves, and act as if it's indeed important to you. Or when you develop an artifact, ask for feedback about it, though not because a process tells you to check the "Peer Reviewed" box; you do it because you realize that feedback (even if it's unpleasant) can help you improve your results.

A shortcut for this second path is to make a change at higher levels than your target one. In the case of mind-set, that means changing something at the role or identity level. If you truly shift your role from manager to leader, from product manager to voice of the business, from marketer to educator of customers, the mind-set will follow. Such shifts, however, don't happen easily; they often require triggers such as inspirational, tragic, near-miss, or "I've-had-enough" experiences.

Conditions for Change

Like any change, a mind-set change requires motivation, bandwidth, and focus.[2] Motivation arises from the intended benefits of Agile and from the shortcomings of the present state. Bandwidth means that you have the time to practice and the slack to reflect on your practice. Focus means having dedicated, undistracted blocks of time for such practice and learning.

For the particular change of an Agile transformation, you'll need high doses of motivation, bandwidth, and focus. Coming back from a conference excited about other companies' success stories might give motivation to *you*, but not necessarily to others who will experience the shift. Limiting the bandwidth of your early iteration retrospectives to 15 minutes because there's always a close deadline means you won't learn how a retrospective really makes a difference. And if your team is constantly in firefighting mode, they won't be able to focus on a change no matter how appealing the target state.

A company engaged me to guide an Agile makeover. When I came in for the first step — an assessment — I found that its new senior leadership had been putting the development teams through the wringer to get a product version out. However, the executives had promised that the pace would relent soon, and I observed that everyone, from individual contributor to site manager, was motivated to improve their lot. A few weeks later I trained the teams, but coaching was put on hold: the executives decided on a strategic change and, to accomplish their new goal, they micromanaged the teams' work for another three months. Coaching started midway through that quarter, but the deck was stacked against its success. Everyone was spent and, what's worse, they had no trust left in their executives.

Every person affected by an Agile transformation needs to understand what they're changing *to*. This basic knowledge is alarmingly missing from many implementations. If you randomly sample technology workers whose management has taken a shine to Agile, and ask them what Agile *is*, you'll probably hear at least one of the following answers:

+ "Agile is this daily meeting where we report status."

+ "Agile is a process with cross-functional teams in which every member can work on anything."

+ "Agile is writing requirements on sticky notes and moving them across a whiteboard."

+ "Agile is when you write code quickly and don't have to design it."

+ "Agile means using X to deliver projects" (X being the name of an Agile planning tool).

+ "Agile is doing things better, cheaper, faster."

These answers conflate Agile with practices, process, tools, mechanics, and intended benefits. Such misunderstanding doesn't only imply that people adopt the wrong thing; it paints Agile in an undesirable light. After all, to team members, the first answer is not attractive, the next three seem risky, and the last two ring like empty marketing promises. When people correctly understand that the objective is a different, whole-system approach to work, their motivation to make the change is accurate. And if that motivation is low, at least you can have an informed conversation with them and discuss the real issues.

People working together in teams and organizations have cultures and subcultures. Culture rewards its followers with a sense of belonging and preserves a power structure. The Agile values are a good fit for some cultures and a threat to others. The farther away your starting point is from an Agile culture, the longer, scarier, and more arduous the change. Sometimes there are catalysts to faster change: impending doom, a charismatic leader, or enough influential people who won't take the status quo anymore.

If you have a different mind-set now, shifting to the Agile one may take several months to several years. There is no clear-cut end state, and the journey will be rocky.[3] You will need patience for the learning experience and enough slack for frequent introspection. You will need the support and patience of others who depend on you or hold you accountable for results. The timing of change, which is a matter of value and potential downside, is important. Breaking down the journey to multiple legs seems to help, especially in large organizations.

Process Design

Let's say you want to apply the Agile mind-set to the work at hand. You need a process — a practical description of how work gets done from idea to delivered result. Where do you get that process?

One option is to start with a clean slate: design a process that embodies the mind-set and respects your context. This option isn't too popular because it's hard work that most people neither are used to nor care for. They just want to get on with *doing* what they're good at, which rarely includes process design and adaptation based on empirical data (merely reading this sentence might cause them vertigo). Throw in the complication that process design is a systems thinking problem, and you've lost them. That's one reason why, in most retrospectives of most teams, deep suggestions for improvement are few and far between.

If there's any leeway in the assignment of people to teams, you'll also need to consider team design. Beyond the obvious criterion of having the necessary skills and abilities to finish valuable work, remember that these people will be working *together*. Some combinations can work out well and yield higher collective intelligence, whereas others may bomb due to interpersonal tension. Give the social/emotional dimension of your staff at least the same amount of attention as you do to their technical skills.

As part of an Agile makeover, a project team of almost 20 was going to separate into three teams (still working with a single product owner). Even though the VP had come up with a suggested team responsibility and assignment structure, he agreed to let me facilitate an exercise in which everyone would self-select into one of the three teams.

Sticky notes with names and key skills went up on the whiteboard. Discussions started. The first two rounds ended in an impasse. To break the tension, one guy said, laughing, "Why don't we just pick the people we want to work with, and then decide which areas those teams will work on?" To which I answered, "Let's try that!" People were noticeably more engaged and less nervous now. They were moving names around, having intense conversations, and looking at the big picture.

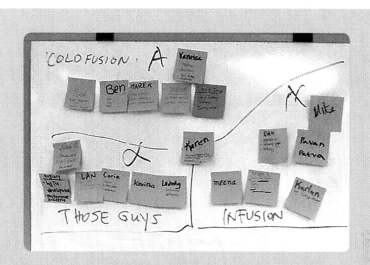

Within 10 minutes we had wonderful, balanced teams of six people each. They chose team names, and later that day chose new desk locations so they could sit together. This new structure made it easier for each individual to adapt to their restarted Agile journey.

Even if you have dozens of teams, you can still evolve a process that respects the Agile mind-set. Assign responsibilities to teams in a way that satisfies the values and principles. The Agile principles all apply when scaling to multiple teams, although some might play out differently at the interteam level than at the intrateam level. Related teams might even follow a different process as long as they all share the mind-set.

If Agile isn't your specialty, you could engage a consultant who specializes in Agile process design. They would assess your current state, tailor a process and choose starter practices for your team, and train the team to use them (obvious disclosure: this is what I do for a living). The critical piece is the assessment; companies that skip it tend to end up with generic, ill-fitting training and processes.

A bank started a two-year data consolidation project with about 30 people. They took interest in Agile, but their environment was still strongly rooted in Waterfall thinking; the process they customized — only for development and QA — was in essence Waterfall with three-week cycles.

The process performed relatively well during the easy first phase of the project, but it was a risk going into the longer, complex second phase. I facilitated a series of collaborative meetings in which 14 key project members designed their approach to phase two. They identified the values and beliefs of that phase, agreed on a set of operating principles (a mix of Agile and Lean), reorganized the subteams, and defined a new process. Neither the team structure nor the new process resembled any documented implementation of Agile or Lean that I'm aware of, but it's what they needed to achieve the objectives of that phase.[4]

The most popular option by far is to pick an established framework, such as Scrum or SAFe. This tactic seems easy (it's documented), cheap (buy books or train a few people), and effective (others say they love it). While there are several Agile frameworks, picking the right framework for your situation is harder than it looks. They don't all emphasize the same principles; Scrum, for instance, has no explicit guidance on simplicity or sustainable pace.[5] Every framework allows a different level of flexibility when it comes to practices and structure, so their power or suitability to your situation are hard to judge. The frameworks may make excellent *starting points*, but they don't eliminate your process design problem; you must still apply their guidance on continuous improvement to adapt them to your context.

Practices

When people have a repeated or customary way of doing something, we call that a practice. Two examples of practices are writing user stories with acceptance criteria, and sitting with a teammate to review your work. Processes describe steps for getting work done; practices describe particular ways to execute each step. Both processes and practices may rely on tools. Once you have a process, the next obvious question is: Which practices and tools to use?

Beware the trap of combining "tried-and-true" Waterfall practices with Agile ones, which often results in failure or mediocrity. A common example is when a team prioritizes and estimates many backlog items and then turns them into a predictive project plan by slotting them into the next five or 10 iterations all at once. You cannot expect to succeed by using practices that support contradictory values, beliefs, or principles. Choose one mind-set, then pick any commonly used practices and techniques, or fashion new ones, that are congruent with that mind-set.

You might look around and ask what others are doing that seems to work well. The trap people fall into at this point is looking for "best" practices, irrespective of context. They might do so as a shortcut to efficiency and correctness, or because they don't know how to start, or because the practices have the blessing of an authority figure. However, this attempt to imitate other people's success creates a downward spiral. Here is why.

If a practice is a bad fit or improperly implemented, it won't achieve its stated purpose. It will even hinder the team, because they won't do something useful instead. For instance, pair programming without an agreed-on framework of expectations may well waste programmers' time.

If people don't understand the purpose of a practice, they will actively resist it, or merely not play along. Take for instance the "Daily

Scrum." This brief daily meeting is meant to facilitate the team's progress toward their iteration goal and commitments. The basic format is for participants to stand in a circle and for each to answer the same three progress-related questions. While it might be a good first attempt at a coordination mechanism, it's rarely "best." Many teams see only the format, not the purpose, so they consider the meeting a nuisance and an interruption. They act accordingly, rendering the meeting ineffective. Unsurprisingly, responding with coercion (such as establishing penalties for no-shows and late arrivals) doesn't help.

In my experience, teams that take these shortcuts to Agile don't usually know or understand the mind-set. They assume that Agile is a process, and when those so-called "best" practices fail to yield results, they conclude that Agile doesn't work. Because those practices are considered best, they don't try to change them; they just keep repeating them, achieving the same results.

To avoid this vicious cycle, resist the temptation of the best practice in the first place. Look around for ideas, and *always* evaluate them for your context. You don't really have a choice, since you work with human beings — not "resources" — and they will ultimately do whatever *they* want, not what someone else's process tells them to do. Since Agile prefers effective to efficient, start there: collaborate with your team to devise methods that seem to yield the right results, not just fast results. Establish feedback loops to know how right the results are and how well the team worked together. As frequently as practical in your situation, improve matters based on that feedback.

Getting Better

Having fulfilled the conditions for change and crafted your strategy and starting point, several tactics will help you adopt the mind-set and develop its associated skills and behaviors. Here are the top tactics, as applied to the Agile experience.

Engage in deliberate practice. Be Agile-minded as you perform daily activities. Don't merely repeat certain actions until they become habit; reflect on your results, receive feedback and coaching from others (even if they are just a few steps ahead of you), and keep challenging yourself.[6]

Learn together. Work with others who are in a similar situation. For example, if you're new to Agile servant leadership, meet regularly with your counterparts in other teams to share stories and reflect together. If you're the product owner and not used to decomposing large work, ask a couple of team members to join you. Fortunately, Agile is a team thing, so growing Agility is also a team responsibility — you're not alone.

Get a coach and a mentor. Coaching is a powerful force of growth and change. It makes the experience easier, increases options, and averts potential disasters. It increases your confidence and likelihood of success through feedback and accountability. Both coaching and mentoring will help you close conscious gaps (what you know that you don't know) as well as unconscious gaps (what you don't know that you don't know).

> On and off since 2006, I've engaged personal coaches or participated in group coaching programs for periods as long as one year. At a substantial investment, they have helped me grow into new professional roles, adjust my values and shed some limiting beliefs, and go further than I'd expected. I consider that money well spent.

Go for quick wins. Success is a powerful catalyst to growth; allow yourself to succeed frequently, even on a small scale. For instance, experiment with time-boxing on your next task by setting a timer for 30 or 60 minutes. Try focusing within that time-box by preventing interruptions like email and phone.[7] Practice getting to "Done" by splitting the task into small *meaningful* pieces — rather than merely being busy or making your best effort — and by finishing even one piece within that time-box. Repeat the above a few times and keep track of your successes. Similarly, new Agile teams set themselves up for a quick win by planning their first iteration around relatively little scope, so they are likely to finish it.

Take it easy. You won't achieve perfection for a while, so set your expectations accordingly. Try to be true to the mind-set, not to a specific "best practice." If your managers expect amazing performance in the early stages, remind them of the learning curve. If they expect great results because they're betting the farm on Agile, they might want to reconsider the timing. Remember, you have to gain practice in quiet times so you're ready for turbulent times.

Be Agile outside of work. Many of the mind-set's elements may apply in your personal life, which may offer a good source of motivation, bandwidth, and focus. Many of the "Individuals and Interactions" principles apply to your relationships with your significant other and your children, and in fact align with some modern parenting and schooling philosophies.[8] Moving from being busy and preoccupied to seeing the value in everything you do will invigorate you. Keeping things simple can save you a lot of time. Being adaptive, rather than set in your ways, can and will affect your relationships. Indeed, if you espouse Agile values and principles in your personal life and then bring them to work, you're likely to feel more authentic and aligned with the experience of a work-related Agile transformation.

SUPPLEMENTARY RESOURCE: Download "Considerations for Choosing Your Agile Coach" from the book's companion website, **www.TheAgileMindsetBook.info**.

How Agile Are You?

If you decide to embrace the mind-set as described in this book, and follow the advice in this chapter, how do you know when your transformation is over, that "you've arrived"?

Many senior managers like to pose this question, which is a problematic one. The transformation isn't a start-middle-and-end type of activity. Individuals, teams, and organizations can never be *done* adopting Agile, just as you can't become a responsible person once and for all. You can only put your mind to it and improve gradually. As you improve, the instances in which you'd want to act with an Agile mind-set, but find that you aren't doing so, will be fewer and farther between.

In this light, the question to ask is about *progress*. Along the (neverending) journey, you can ask, "How Agile *are* we?" In more practical terms, the first question to ask is: "Do we truly espouse the Agile values and beliefs?" And since mind-set translates into action, the next question is: "Do our behaviors reflect the Agile principles?" Let's start with the latter.

The following table poses specific questions you can use to evaluate your application of the principles. These questions have you examine your "state of Agile" along a scale, rather than in black-or-white, "do-we-or-don't-we?" terms. You might choose to come up with precise metrics for some of them. Or, you could invoke Agile's simplicity principle and devise informal, discrete scales or qualitative measures.

PRINCIPLE	QUESTION
Respect	How well do we respect others and their contribution?
Transparency	How accessible is the information that guides our decisions and actions?
Trust	To what extent do we rely on each other to act professionally, predictably, and with integrity?
Personal Safety	How much useful input do people offer without fear of retribution?
Focus	How frequently are we able to concentrate on our work and bring it closer to completion?
Sustainable Pace	All things being equal, how long can the team continue delivering value at our current level of effort?
Self-Organizing Teams	How much, and how well, do we distribute work among ourselves?
Collaboration	How much positive synergy does our team have?
Communication	How informed are people when they approach a task that depends on others?
Consensus	How effectively does our team make, implement, and support decisions?
Leadership	How trusting, supportive, and humane is the environment in which our team operates?
Outcome	How outcome-minded are people when they perform their tasks?
Effective	How much more attention do we pay to doing the *right* things than to doing them quickly?
Defer	How well do we identify the last responsible moment for making decisions, and how close to that moment do we make them?
Simplicity	How much work are we able to avoid without negative consequences?
Experiment	How well, fast, and cheap do we learn about what's right and what works?

PRINCIPLE	QUESTION
Cadence	How close is our delivery frequency to the frequency that our business needs and can sustain?
Reliability	How reliably do we deliver value now, and how well do we avoid compromising our future ability to deliver value?
Cost of Change	How well do we control the cost of change (where it matters)?
Shippable	How often is our product in a working and shippable (releasable) state?
Quality	Do we regularly pay quality and technical excellence the attention they need to support our goals?
Time-Box	How useful are our time-boxes to meeting our objectives? How well do we adhere to the time-boxes?
Results	How focused are we on value delivery, learning, or risk reduction?
Feedback	How short, useful, and *used* are our feedback loops?
Learning	As time goes on, how much better do we know ourselves, our work, and our customers?
Improvement	How often do we improve our process and teamwork? And our product?

These questions explore solely the application of the Agile mind-set, as opposed to the team's performance or the benefits from Agile, which are different matters. The questions will help you avoid two common mistakes of measuring Agility:

1. Quantifying process compliance. A team might be following every documented Scrum practice, for instance, and still have taken on little of the mind-set.

2. Asking "What's our velocity?" (and subsequently "Can we increase it?"). Velocity measures a team's capacity to produce

output. It is not a measure of the Agility of their behavior or of the usefulness of their output. It's not even a good measure of the benefits of Agile.

This is not to say that you shouldn't measure performance or business benefits. If you do, choose metrics that don't run afoul of the Agile mind-set. The most common faux pas in that regard is to rank and compare staff based on their accomplishment of individual work goals. In too many teams, this performance management approach subverts team-based planning and completing valuable work together.

If you and your fellow team members seem to follow the principles, there's a good likelihood that you also live by the values. Check that by asking about each of the Agile values, "How well do we abide by it?" If some of the answers surprise you, that's a clue that something's amiss. Call a team meeting and discuss collaboratively how to make things better — that's the Agile thing to do.

SUPPLEMENTARY RESOURCE: Download the "How Agile Are You?" worksheet from the book's companion website, **www.TheAgileMindsetBook.info**.

Management

Managers are key to any organization's growth, adaptation, and accomplishments. If you're a manager in an organization that decides to embrace Agile, you're part of the transformation. You're far more than a participant; your natural role in the transformation is that of a leader. You shine a light on the destination — even if it's new to you as well. You spend extra effort to make sure that the destination is correctly understood, mindfully chosen, and clearly communicated. You support people along the journey, particularly by maintaining an environment that welcomes the learning and doesn't penalize normal setbacks (you "make it safe to fail").

"One thing that comes up a lot is convincing people what it means to be successful. To get them thinking about what's valuable, about actually finishing work, and out of their head space of 'If I do my part well, everything is going to work out great.' To always think about the customer perspective."

– Nick Oddson, Senior Vice President, Product Development, D2L

In the early days of the Agile movement, *courage* was said to be one of the Agile values.[9] The inclusion of courage was intended to allow Agile team members to speak up, reach out, tell the truth, warn, do the right thing, respond, adapt, and stand by their decisions. In other words, to practice Agile — which is anchored in four other values altogether.* Courage, then, is an *enabler*, a key part of making the culture change possible. That change is where managers take a leading role.** Their courage — better yet, their fearlessness — to speak up, educate, push back, champion, empower, and otherwise take a stand for the desired target culture is key to bringing it about. That is leadership; true leaders, in fact, have a greater span of influence than their title and position imply.

A common managerial mistake is to "inflict Agile" on staff. With the best of intents, managers re-form teams, change titles around, procure tools and training, and expect teams to delight at being empowered. This story rarely ends well because of its inherent contradiction: managers use their positional authority over individuals to organize them into teams, where they are supposed to *self-organize* and hold each other accountable — voluntarily. One reason for this mistake is seeing Agile merely as process, tools, and practices for achieving

---

* That is why I have not included courage among the values, beliefs, and principles in chapter 1.

** This is particularly true of middle managers, who tend to be the force behind actual organizational change and reinvention.[10]

better results. The other reason is the belief that Agile would improve performance and daily experience, so the team would naturally love it. Sometimes this happens, but a manager would do better to first stoke the motivation and willingness ("create buy-in") for working with such a mind-set. Without that motivation, the team will come along for the ride because they are obliged to; they might "do Agile," possibly quite poorly.

Another common mistake is to establish an objective of *doing* Agile: to have the cross-functional teams, roles, iterations, artifacts, meetings, lingo, "best practices," and tools. Yet none of these elements make you Agile if the foundation is missing. Getting to "doing Agile" may sometimes work as an interim milestone on the way to an overall mind-set change. Throughout that journey, which takes a while, keep reminding yourself *why* you're using these methods and structures, and taking a principled approach.

These two strategies — inflicting Agile, and settling for "doing Agile" — are rarely effective, but at least they are mindful. I've come across many senior managers who picked a third way, setting the following expectation: "I don't care about your methods, as long as you deliver." This strategy looked terrific: the trusting managers empowered their teams to choose their process. However, those managers never created a true Agile environment where its benefits accrued. Their teams went through the Agile motions — some truly attempting to follow the principles — but did not integrate well with the rest of the organization, which continued to live by non-Agile values: minimize cost and schedule, commit early, get it right the first time, minimize change. An organization that wishes to have only some of its units use Agile must establish an Agile-friendly business and management atmosphere in those units.

If you're a functional or team manager, a move to Agile will change your work drastically. Your subordinates will now be part of a cross-functional team; their allegiance will be primarily to their teammates; they will negotiate their work plan with someone else. More than manage workers, you will lead and coach them; more than managing activities, you will help remove obstacles to organizational Agility. You will have a greater effect on the culture; some of that will be due to changes in your people-management activities, especially hiring and performance management.

> "Transforming my mind-set from a manager to a servant leader was (and still is) hard. My main goals are to assist the team in every possible way, to reduce their distractions, and to help remove any impediments they may encounter. Two principles guide me in 'moments of weakness':
>
> 1. Be committed to the outcome but not attached to the way.
> 2. Ask questions, rather than tell team members what to do or how to do it."
>
> *– Alon Sabi, CTO at Function Point Productivity Software*

Many managers find these changes daunting, all the more so if their own superiors still expect business-as-usual, non-Agile practices. I've seen managers respond to this turmoil by resisting Agile and limiting team autonomy. This response, self-preserving though it seems to be, isn't good long-term for either the business or the manager. A better response is to support and empower the team, becoming a servant leader in the process. Managers who do that typically report that sometimes their organization got more than it expected, so they have extra responsibilities now: partner across the organization, coach their peers and superiors, and promote organizational Agility. For some, the personal growth potential involved in that is huge.

I wish I could tell you that adopting the Agile mind-set is simple and easy. It's neither. The required change, especially in business settings, is pervasive; it takes education, patience, leadership, and cultural adaptation. Make sure you understand what you're getting yourself (and others) into. Be mindful about your choices; resist the temptation to simply adopt a framework and to imitate others' success. Improve continuously. This is indeed a lot of work, but making the Agile promise happen may turn out to be the most fulfilling part of your career.

APPENDIX A

The Waterfall Mind-Set Compared to the Agile One

For decades, the reigning paradigm for managing software development work has been Waterfall. In fact, it has been so ubiquitous that until Agile came along, many practitioners didn't know that their methodology was *called* Waterfall. Borrowed from manufacturing industries, this linear and sequential life cycle model was developed to address the particular needs and activities of software development, such as requirements, design, programming, and testing. Here are the values, beliefs, and principles that make up the Waterfall mind-set.

Values

The Waterfall mind-set is anchored in four foundational values. Meaning, if you choose the Waterfall approach for the work at hand, your top-ranked values in the situation include, and don't contradict, the following (in no particular order):

+ **Make early commitments.** The people doing the work ought to commit to its recipient that they would deliver a specific result with high quality by a certain date and within a certain budget.

+ **Get it right the first time.** The recipient and the provider ought to understand the solution well enough for the provider

177

to create it in a single, efficient pass. Changes to the work ought to be minimal, early, and closely controlled.

✦ **Deliver on time and on budget.** Success means meeting the commitments, particularly those of cost and schedule.

✦ **Process comes first, before product and before people.** There ought to be standardized processes for specifying and delivering the required product, regardless of who executes them. Success shouldn't be affected if the "human resources" who do the work are replaced by others who have the right business and technical skills.

As a set, these values contradict the Agile ones on several dimensions. For instance, Waterfall wants to eliminate uncertainty, while Agile expects it and prepares to handle it. That's not to say that one set is right and the other is wrong; they merely apply in different contexts. If I'm a restaurant chef, designing the menu to include a $25 Penne Alla Vodka is an early commitment. Once a seated guest orders it, I'd better prepare it right the first time and within an acceptable time frame. If my restaurant is to survive, a standardized process for buying ingredients, storing them, and preparing dishes would ensure a sufficient profit margin. On the other hand, if a marketing specialist is developing a new campaign for my restaurant, both of us would benefit from close collaboration, adaptability, and early results.

Note in particular the different fundamental approach to the customer of the work. While Agile doesn't believe that the customer is always right, it places a premium on adaptation and customer collaboration to make sure that the team works on *what's right for the customer*. Therefore, the nature and content of the work may change, perhaps even radically, before it's presumably done. Waterfall, by contrast, values predictability, so it's okay to deliver results only at major milestones, which may be months or years apart; there is no expectation of changing any customer's experience midway.

Beliefs

While both Agile and Waterfall are anchored in only four values, each mind-set has at least a dozen beliefs and assumptions about the work, the workers, and the customer. Here are Waterfall's. (For your reference, the Agile beliefs are in chapter 1.)

Waterfall work typically starts with elicitation of the customer's requirements and getting sign-off on them. This is justified by the beliefs that the customer knows what she wants, and we can get that effectively out of her head. In fact, upfront requirement elicitation and product design are critical for the customer's satisfaction, since what we determine now will remain valuable and mostly unchanged when it's delivered.

In Waterfall, a top value is to get the solution right the first time. Bolstering this value are several beliefs, first among which is that *it's possible to do so*. It's also possible to determine a correct and practical design for the solution. Moreover, it's possible to predetermine all the important tasks, and planning is an appropriate response to the complexity of product development.

Planning doesn't just address complexity, according to Waterfall; it substantiates commitments, especially around schedule and cost. After all, changes are costly, and the cost explodes in the later stages of the game. Efficiency is gained by analyzing the functional activities and organizing the people for focused performance and minimal expenditure. Effectiveness is a given: if each function team, such as analysis, specification, design, and construction, performs competently, the end result will satisfy the customers. Big-bang verification and user acceptance testing at the end *should not* uncover too many critical faults.

Since Waterfall values standardized processes and thus standardized work, the corresponding belief is that an effective and efficient process can be determined up front and kept static. The people who apply the process can be viewed as resources, interchangeable as long as they have the right skills. If they do overtime, they will produce additional valuable results. They can, and will, document their actions and knowledge in a useful manner for later consumption by others who might replace them. Managers determine what the workers do, and that's an efficient approach to meeting commitments. And when skilled resources (meaning people) are in short supply, spreading them across projects is not only manageable, it's also a good way to minimize costs and time.

Just as the set of four Agile values contradicts the Waterfall ones, their beliefs don't agree, either. An all-too-common antipattern is for people to learn about the Agile values and declare their importance to them — all the while retaining the Waterfall beliefs. As chapter 9 explains, beliefs support values, so a person's (or team's, or organization's) *real* set of top values will guide their actions.

Principles

The one metaprinciple of Waterfall is to organize the work sequentially. In this sequence, running all the way from idea to delivered result, each stage involves a set of related activities that culminate with artifacts that get passed down to the next stage.

Whereas almost half of Agile's principles have to do with people, Waterfall has only two in that regard. The first is to consider work-ers as "resources," meaning that successful execution requires solely technical skills. The second is to organize workers in function-based teams corresponding to the sequence of stages, and to have them communicate with other functions through managers and leads.

Waterfall work follows three principles for achieving business objectives. Have a single person take responsibility for the entire work; additional individuals may take responsibility for intermediate stages. Manage constraints according to the Iron Triangle: of cost, schedule, and scope, nail down two and vary the third (otherwise quality would suffer). And as work proceeds, use sign-offs: have authorized parties review completed artifacts and approve that they are in fact complete, so there's no need to revisit them.

In terms of making the work count, Waterfall calls for specialists and "working the plan." Before starting, involve specialists in preparing a correct, efficient plan for the work. During execution, produce the correct deliverables in one pass by having specialists carry out the plan's tasks.

Since the plan is the primary vehicle for delivering on early commitments, Waterfall includes three principles for tight execution according to the plan. Use the "hub and spokes" organizational pattern: entrust certain people with optimizing work allocation and coordinating workers' activities. Maximize each worker's utilization — keep them maximally busy. And once authorized entities have signed off on the plan, limit changes to it.

Given Agile's orientation toward people, you might hear Agilists refer to Waterfall as a "command and control" paradigm. While nothing in the four Waterfall values actually calls for *controlling* or *commanding* workers, the beliefs and principles do make this possible. And when the values are accompanied (or even driven) by anxiety over the unknown or the uncertain, people will opt for methods that seem to control the unknown and the uncertain. I have indeed observed that, in Waterfall projects that were not fear-based, managers implemented the principles in a way that did not overly command or control people.

APPENDIX B

Examples

How I Used Agile to Renovate a House

Home renovations typically require coordination among multiple tradespeople, who often also have other jobs on the go. The substantial money involved in renos comes out of the homeowners' pockets, who then have to live with the results for several years.

Renovation contractors like to approach their work with the Waterfall mind-set. First, the homeowners make a list of renovation items and negotiate a price. Given the scope of work, the contractor manages the project to minimize cost and schedule, intending to maximize their profit margin and get to the next job sooner. Everything is written down and trust is not assumed.

This approach, while good in theory, often ends badly for both parties. When costs exceed the estimate due to construction realities, conflicts typically arise and both sides take a financial hit. Inevitable delays disrupt the homeowners' life and delay the contractor's next job. It's not unusual for contractors to leave jobs before they end and to not be paid for 100% of the work.

What if you're a new homeowner, you have a two-month deadline for renovations and little knowledge about the subject matter, and money's tight? This was my wife and me in 2003, three months before our firstborns came along (yes, twins). Controlling cost and schedule was important to us, but even more so, we wanted to feel good about living in the house after the renos. So we found Barry, a contractor we could trust, and worked out a shared vision and an Agile-minded process with him.

We started by listing the 19 changes we wanted. Barry was going to order our list according to dependencies and efficiencies and then quote us the entire job. We asked instead for an itemized quote: how much each item would cost on its own, and how much that cost would drop if it were done after another item.

Then my wife and I had a conversation, which frequently featured the phrases "We're not going to need *that*" (i.e., YAGNI) and "*This can wait*." Together with Barry we decided on two phases: six items would be done in phase 1, before the move, and three would be done in phase 2, between the move and the births. At that point we'd established a good relationship with him, and could be clear about budget and schedule limitations, and possible tradeoffs.

Starting with big, important items, phase 1 work generally proceeded one item at a time. Every two days, my wife and I visited the house to see progress. Even though we preferred to make decisions together, we agreed that to move the work along, one of us could make a binding decision. We were both available to Barry (at least on the phone) for information, inspection, and corrective action. There were surprises all the time, such as a new doorway that couldn't be as wide as we'd thought, and the silliest reason causing us to get new fixtures for the master bathroom. Small and large changes were the norm.

Our contractor was open and helpful, and didn't waste time, but phase 1 still ran late. We had to postpone our move by a few days, which meant extra costs. By the time we moved in, most of our initial budget was spent, so we cut items from phase 2. Living in the house, we discovered additional necessary fixes, and added some for which we still had money and time.

A few weeks later the renovations were officially over, and we celebrated with a house-warming party. This turned out to be good timing, since five days later the twins were born.

In hindsight, one of the nine items didn't justify the time and money we spent on it. Four of the postponed 10 items turned out to be wholly unnecessary. Barry, with whom we'd established a solid relationship, completed the remaining six items when we could afford the time and hassle. Rather than cramming them into the initial project, or ruling them out altogether, treating these items as "we might get to them someday" helped my wife and me — the customers — contain our costs, retain some of our sanity, and welcome our babies to a pleasant home just in time.

Unscripted Collaboration

An important Agile belief is that collaboration — two brains on a task — generally yields a higher-quality outcome than those two brains working separately on two tasks. This personal story demonstrates how collaboration can result in innovation.

A few years ago, a conference accepted my proposal for a new full-day session on advanced Agility. In its abstract, I promised an experiential, PowerPoint-free workshop. My normal procedure for any teaching experience is to design it myself, then have colleagues and my wife, Ronit — who has a different professional background than mine — review my design. Apply their feedback, review, repeat until done.

At some point, I sat down to design the workshop. As it happens, Ronit was home sick that day, and she agreed to design the workshop with me.

For the first 30 minutes, I did most of the talking. We reviewed the workshop's "target persona," its promised outcome, and the topics I hoped to cover. And then we said, "Let's develop a simulation for the attendees."

We had *no clue* how to get started. We stared at the whiteboard for a while. Ronit offered, "Tell me about the simulations you experienced at AYE" (Jerry Weinberg's *Amplifying Your Effectiveness* conference).

I recounted some experiences and that gave us an idea. We elaborated on it. Some aspects of the simulation felt good; what we wanted the participants to do felt awkward.

Still, we made progress. It looked like a conversation in front of a whiteboard, with occasional peeking at my laptop for more data. And then something funny happened.

Ronit, who does paper crafts for a hobby, was scheduled to teach a recycling-craft workshop to teens the next day. Our conversation had shifted to discussing whether she'd go, as she was still sick. I was thinking, "Well, she could also choose to run a simulation with the kids, so she wouldn't have to talk much." To make my point without words, I gestured at the whiteboard. She misunderstood the gesture and said, "You mean we could have the simulation participants do this craft?"

I stared at her. My workshop attendees would be software project managers. This particular craft relies heavily on paper and masking tape. I would *never* have suggested it. Neither would she, if she hadn't been involved in this design. Even if she had offered this idea, I would have dismissed it (politely). But that morning, my mind was receptive.

We laughed at the misunderstanding and dove into exploring her idea. It was absolutely *perfect*. We sketched it out. We went for a walk during which we elaborated on it some more. Ideas, extensions, and modifications were just flying. In the afternoon, she demonstrated making some artifacts and we made sure our attendees could pull them off. After a total of four hours, we were done.

Working alone, I might have taken the same amount of time. I can't imagine that alternative outcome and whether it would have been as unusual, exhilarating, and fun — and such a hit in the actual workshop. Ronit would have spent that time doing something on her own; afterward, she would have reviewed my ideas. Apply feedback, repeat.

Instead, we produced a quality workshop. We had fun, shared an experience, and learned creative ideas from each other. A few things certainly helped, and they are true of any collaboration:

✦ I didn't dominate by saying, "This is *my* task. I need to design this workshop. I welcome your opinions and ideas, but I'll decide." It was a symmetrical experience.

✦ We began with the end in mind. Our process was fluid. We allowed ourselves to get off track and to take breaks (one was to make soup, one was to take a walk). The changes in perspective helped both of us.

✦ We made the time and were fully present in the design session. If she had said, "I can only spare an hour," we wouldn't have reached this outcome.

Mindful Process Design

As explained in chapter 1, the choice of processes and methods must follow the determination of the mind-set: values, beliefs, and principles. While this book is focused on the particulars of the Agile mind-set, this mindful approach to process design applies across other contexts and mind-sets. Here are two examples.

The Work: Clearing Snow from the Driveway

It's a cold February morning in my city, Toronto, with the temperature at −15°C (5°F). At 8:10 a.m., I need to drive the kids to school. The car is inside the garage, but the driveway is covered by 15cm (6 inches) of fresh snow. I won't be back home until 6 p.m.

I have certain values and beliefs around driving in these winter conditions:

✦ I value keeping the driveway clear of snow and ice (which makes it safely navigable).

✦ I believe that if I drive the car on that layer of snow in the driveway, it could get stuck.

✦ I also believe that if the snow is untouched (or driven over) by the evening, it will turn bumpy and the top layer will turn to ice. The longer I wait, the harder it will be to remove.

This is not the end of the story, since the time of day and other obligations also affect my mind-set. Here are two common scenarios.

Scenario A

The time is 8 a.m. Keeping the driveway safely navigable is still important to me, but what's *more* important to me is to get the kids to school on time.

Since I only have 10 minutes, I choose the principle "effective over efficient." I will plow only two narrow tracks of snow, wide enough for the car's tires. This picture shows me 75% of the way through the task:

I will still have to finish the work when I'm back home in the evening. It will probably be harder than if I did it right the first time, but I'm focused on accomplishing more-important goals.

Scenario B

The time is 7:10 a.m., and I have a whole hour to dedicate to the driveway. Since this is ample time for clearing it completely, I know I'll do a proper job. I do, however, want to spend the least time in the cold doing this backbreaking task.

Therefore, I choose the principles of efficiency and safety. I will plan my activities before starting, and my plan will account for the following:

✦ Where I'd like the snow piles to be when I'm done

✦ How to eliminate unnecessary motion

✦ How to minimize the need to lift a full shovel

The Work: Serving Lunch

Every weekday, office workers need to eat lunch, usually around the same time. Feeding those who didn't bring lunch from home presents a business opportunity. In Western cities, the typical options fall into two categories: fast-food places, either take-away or sit-down, and restaurants, either take-out or sit-down. What is the food providers' mind-set regarding the work of serving lunch?

I suppose that most food establishment have similar values around profit and repeat business. Fancier restaurants, as well as chains, have values around ambience and concept. All of them seem to believe that customers like a variety of hot options. Where fast-food places seem to differ from restaurants is in their belief about the customer's needs and expectations. Fast food is built on the premise that customers have no time to waste, so two of their principles are to order at the cash register and to offer no table service (some don't even have tables). To address variety, their principle is to allow combinations of basic options. On the other hand, most regular restaurant owners seem to believe that their customers want the sit-down, table-service experience, so they offer that and pay less attention to speed of service.

One popular Thai restaurant in downtown Toronto seems to operate as if they hold both beliefs. Their lunchtime principles include
rapid table service, frequent menu updates, quality cooking, and
offering combinations of premade dishes. Whenever I go there, the
hostess is quick to seat my party and hand us the lunch menu. Every
week that menu is different, but it always has eight main dishes (one
chicken, one tofu, and so on). I can order any one of them for the same
price, or any two for a higher price; they always come with the same
sides, and they cost the same as the fast-food equivalent. All eight are
made right before lunch and still taste fresh. The server materializes
quickly and and it's rarely longer than three minutes before he returns
with the plates. But if I order from the regular menu, I'll have to wait
longer. When I'm finished, they are quick to take payment. A recent
lunch there, for instance, took 35 minutes.

Their lunchtime mind-set — giving patrons a quality restaurant
experience at fast-food speed and expense — seems to work for them.
They are always full at lunch and claim to enjoy substantial repeat
business, going on 20 years.

ACKNOWLEDGMENTS

Over the last 10 years, the Agile community has been something of a second home to me. We're not a small community anymore, but we tend to be close. We help each other, congregate at the same conferences, and have conversations virtually all the time. For many of us, helping others benefit from Agile is more than a vocation, it is a unique passion — because its mind-set resonates with us so much. Members of the Agile community, I appreciate you for the good work you do. I continue to learn from you, and I'm glad to share your consensus and my learnings in these pages.

This community wouldn't exist if its early thought leaders hadn't collaborated on defining Agile. Manifesto authors, I am grateful for your pioneering work. You've given the world options, and created for me the best job ever.

Around the world, countless professionals are trying out Agile methods and approaches, discovering how to collaboratively create meaningful deliverables. Keep at it, folks; the world will eventually consider that model the norm, rather than the exception. I thank those of you who have contributed stories to the book, in pursuit of that possibility.

Naturally, the Agile mindset guided me in creating this book, and that included many feedback cycles. As I say in chapter 2, asking for feedback is like going to the doctor. I got to see many empathetic, helpful "doctors" right away: Elizabeth Akagla, Christopher Avery, Ian Brockbank, Sekhar Burra, Paul Carvalho, Guy Dela Marta, John Hill, Dave Jacques, Patrick Li, Adam Myhr, Alan Padula, Ken Rubin, Alon Sabi, Lynn Shrewsbury, Dan Snyder, Mikko Sorvari, Jean Tabaka, and Zuzana Zabkova.

Since I started 3P Vantage in 2009, thousands of professionals like you — or, more often, their organizations — have chosen to attend my workshops and receive my coaching. This is a serious responsibility, and I greatly appreciate you for investing in your growth through me. I continue to learn immensely from my interactions with you. Without your trust in me, this book wouldn't exist.

And finally, the one person without whom this book definitely wouldn't exist is my one and only Ronit. You've freed up so much time and space for me to write. You've reviewed, critiqued, and edited everything I wrote before I dared show it to anyone else. You've consistently supported me with endless patience. Ronit, it is so delightful to spend this lifetime creating with you.

Gil Broza
Toronto, Canada

NOTES

Introduction

1   "Lean" is a mind-set toward work. The best-known example of its earliest application was the Toyota Production System. Since then, Lean has been adapted to development environments. Although its foundational values are different from Agile's, its set of principles bears a striking resemblance to that of Agile, and many Lean software development processes look quite like Agile ones.

Chapter 1

1   The Agile Manifesto, agilemanifesto.org.

2   "Theory X" and "Theory Y" about worker motivation were described in the 1960s. See the Wikipedia entry, en.wikipedia.org/wiki/Theory_X_and_Theory_Y.

3   The Cynefin Framework, en.wikipedia.org/wiki/Cynefin, offers a typology of contexts that guides what sort of explanations or solutions might apply to a problem, situation, or system. It describes five domains, "complex" being one of them. The other four are obvious, complicated, chaotic, and disorder.

4   The Manifesto makes no mention of several principles that are part of Agile today, such as transparency, safety, focus, deferring decisions, and learning. It does touch on other principles, such as servant leadership, quality, and effectiveness, rather indirectly.

5   Stephen R. Covey, *The 7 Habits of Highly Effective People: Powerful Lessons in Personal Change* (Free Press, 2004).

Chapter 2

1   Based on research quoted in "How marriage makes people healthier" in *The Economist*, economist.com/blogs/economist-explains/2015/01/economist-explains-0.

Chapter 3

1   Marcus Hammarberg and Joakim Sunden, *Kanban in Action* (Manning, 2014).

2   James Surowiecki, *The Wisdom of Crowds: Why the Many Are Smarter Than the Few and How Collective Wisdom Shapes Business, Economies, Societies and Nations* (Doubleday, 2004).

Chapter 4

1　See note 2 in chapter 1.

2　This is my paraphrasing of a statement made by Dale Emery.

3　The movie is *Mr. Magorium's Wonder Emporium*, from 2007, www.imdb.com/title/tt0457419/.

4　Accountability may catalyze performance, but it cannot *motivate* people. In particular, never attempt to motivate people by holding them accountable to an estimate. Read more in "Should I Expect Accountability from the Team?," section 10.3 in Gil Broza, *The Human Side of Agile: How to Help Your Team Deliver* (3P Vantage Media, 2012).

5　This is an abbreviation of Norm Kerth's Prime Directive for retrospectives. See endnote 6 to chapter 3 of *The Human Side of Agile*. Also, see "The Best Advice I Ever Got" with Indra Nooyi, Chairperson and CEO of Pepsico, archive.fortune.com/galleries/2008/fortune/0804/gallery.bestadvice.fortune/7.html.

6　Listen to Dianne Marsh from Netflix, infoq.com/presentations/netflix-velocity-tools-culture, and Daniel Schauenberg from Etsy, infoq.com/presentations/development-deployment-collaboration-etsy, describe continuous deployment at their respective companies. The tooling may differ, but the cultural response to its risks and challenges is strikingly similar.

7　Extreme Programming (XP) is one of the earlier Agile methodologies, heavily focused on technical practices for software development. See Kent Beck with Cynthia Andres, *Extreme Programming Explained: Embrace Change*, 2d ed. (Addison-Wesley Professional, 2004).

8　Tom DeMarco, *Slack: Getting Past Burnout, Busywork, and the Myth of Total Efficiency* (Broadway, 2002).

Chapter 5

1　This wording comes from Christopher Avery. Read more about what encourages team members to pull together in *The Human Side of Agile*.

2　"How Should I Form an Agile Team?," section 4.1 in *The Human Side of Agile*.

3　R. Brian Stanfield, *The Workshop Book: From Individual Creativity to Group Action* (ICA series) (New Society Publishers, 2002).

4　This simplified model of group development first appeared in Bruce Tuckman, "Developmental Sequence in Small Groups," *Psychological Bulletin* 63 (1965): 384–99. For more details on the model and its application to Agile teams, see "What Are the Stages of Team Evolution?," section 6.1 in *The Human Side of Agile*.

Chapter 6

1 "Which Impediments Should I Remove?," section 2.4 in *The Human Side of Agile*.

2 Context-Driven Testing was initially developed by James Bach, Brian Marick, Bret Pettichord, and Cem Kaner. Read about it at **context-driven-testing.com**.

3 The Broken Windows theory was first introduced in 1982. The Wikipedia entry for it is at **en.wikipedia.org/wiki/Broken_windows_theory**.

4 "How Does the Team Customize Their Process?," section 6.2 in *The Human Side of Agile*.

5 "Can Specialists Be Team Members?," section 4.3 in *The Human Side of Agile*.

Chapter 7

1 Michael Feathers, *Working Effectively with Legacy Code* (Prentice Hall, 2004).

2 Read **agilemodeling.com/essays/costOfChange.htm** for an explanation of the cost of change curve and of how various development techniques affect it.

3 "Should Team Members Work in Pairs?," section 6.6 in *The Human Side of Agile*.

Chapter 8

1 For more on this, see "Make Continuous Improvement a Reality," chapter 13 in *The Human Side of Agile*.

2 For the universal process that describes human experience through change, see "What Happens to Performance During Change?," section 11.1 in *The Human Side of Agile*.

3 The growth-fixed dichotomy is a person's mind-set about self-development. People with a growth mind-set believe that they always have something to learn and improve; they don't avoid experimentation out of fear of failure. People with a fixed mind-set believe that their basic traits are set in stone and their accomplishments are due to talent; they stick to what they know. See more in Carol Dweck, *Mindset: The New Psychology of Success* (Random House, 2006).

4 "Qualities for a Dynamic Team," section 4.2.3 in *The Human Side of Agile*.

Chapter 9

1 "Why Do Some Changes Stick Better Than Others?," section 11.5 in *The Human Side of Agile*.

2 "What Are the Preconditions for Successful Change?," section 11.3 in *The Human Side of Agile*.

3   "What Happens to Performance During Change?," section 11.1 in *The Human Side of Agile.*

4   If you have a nonstandard project and you'd like me to take your team through this exercise, write to me at **gbroza@3PVantage.com**.

5   "The Scrum Guide," **scrumguides.org**.

6   Geoff Colvin, *Talent Is Overrated: What Really Separates World-Class Performers from Everybody Else* (Portfolio, 2008). Daniel Coyle, *The Talent Code: Greatness Isn't Born. It's Grown. Here's How* (Bantam, 2009).

7   These tips form part of the Pomodoro technique, **pomodorotechnique.com**.

8   A well-known example is Montessori education, **en.wikipedia.org/wiki/Montessori_ education**. My children spent nine years in a Montessori classroom, and their experience bore a strong resemblance to the Agile experience, considering their developmental stage and an educational setting.

9   Specifically, courage is one of the values of Extreme Programming and of Scrum.

10 Tom DeMarco, *Slack: Getting Past Burnout, Busywork, and the Myth of Total Efficiency* (Broadway, 2002).

INDEX

An *n* following a page reference indicates information found in the notes.

A

acceptance
  by customer, 33, 81, 108, 120
  criteria, 37
  testing, 42, 78, 135, 179
accountability, 76, 90, 194n4
adaptation, 6, 9, 13, 49–51, 106, 121, 126, 134, 146, 178
Agile adoption, xviii, 3, 68–69, 148, 153–76
Agile makeover, 155, 160, 162
Agile Manifesto, 6, 10–11, 71,
Agile team leader (ATL), 55, 74, 90, 98–99, 110, 147
assessments, 19, 99, 111, 149, 160, 163
ATDD (acceptance test-driven development), 33, 135
ATL. *See* Agile team leader
autonomy, 88–89, 115, 120, 147

B

backlog, 29–30, 50–53, 57–58, 96
barriers to participation, 75
begin with the end in mind, 12, 20, 76, 78
behaviors
  product features as, 49, 128, 132–34, 141
  micro-, 134–36

of people, 44, 60, 79, 118–19, 122, 146, 158
  renter vs. owner, 90–91
beliefs, 2–4, 7–10, 16, 30–31, 56, 75, 96, 105, 113, 130, 140–41, 154–58, 164, 174, 179–81
best practices, 165–66, 174
"Big Design Up-Front" (BDUF), 37, 126–27, 130
"Boy Scout Rule," 113, 138
buy-in, 78, 148, 174

C

cadence, 13, 46, 54, 68, 150
capabilities, 45, 66, 89, 93, 110, 122, 162
change
  adjusting to, 32, 150, 167
  bandwidth for, 84
  conditions for, 159–61
  cost of, 13, 49–50, 59, 120–22, 124, 126, 137, 140
  experience during, 148–49, 174–75
  Logical Levels of Change, 156–59
  managers' and leaders' role in, 99, 147, 174–75
  mid-iteration, 111
  performance during, 89
  to plans, design, or implementation 22, 47, 53, 68, 127–28, 133

time-box, 14, 43–46, 59, 106, 114
tools, 3, 71, 121, 125, 127, 136, 165, 173
transformation, Agile. *See* Agile
 adoption
transparency, 11, 33, 51, 75, 92, 120
trust, 11, 30, 38, 47, 75, 83, 90, 95, 104,
 107, 120, 160
Tuckman's Group Development model,
 194n4

U
user stories, 24–25, 33, 58, 65, 165
utilization (of people as resources), 13,
 72, 84, 181

V
value (meaning "important thing"),
 2–6, 10, 15–16, 30, 56, 105–6, 126,
 144, 153–54, 156–57, 161, 164, 172–
 73, 177–81
value (meaning "worth"), 13, 24–25,
 53, 95
value delivery, 6–7, 13, 50, 57, 65–66,
 73, 76–77, 88, 93, 107, 111, 128, 151
visibility, 47, 92, 109, 118–20

W
waste, 30, 51, 53, 59, 133, 165
Waterfall, 4, 16, 30–31, 37, 42, 46, 59,
 105, 111, 126, 140, 165, 177–81
work in process (WIP), 110–11, 145
workspace, 97

X
XP. *See* eXtreme Programming

Y
YAGNI (You Aren't Gonna Need It),
 39, 51–53, 184

MEET GIL BROZA

Principal Agile Mentor and Owner,
3P Vantage, Inc.
Email contact: **gbroza@3PVantage.com**

In writing *The Agile Mind-Set*, Gil Broza has addressed an aching need shared by organizations worldwide. As his experience and observations confirm, many who adopt Agile pay too much attention to processes and tools, and end up disenchanted with the results. Some are in denial while some are searching for a magic bullet. Still more are stranded on a mediocre performance plateau, stalled in a mishmash of "best practices," and looking for answers.

In the last 11 years alone, Gil has mentored and coached more than 2,000 professionals who then delighted their customers, shipped working software on time, and rediscovered passion for their work. He has also:

✦ Worked as a development manager, team leader, and programmer for 12 years, successfully applying Agile methods since 2001

✦ Coached dozens of private- and public-sector clients, large and small, including independent software vendors, custom development firms, and IS/IT departments

✦ Served as a regular writer for the prestigious online magazine **projectmanagement.com** (a PMI publication), contributing articles on effective Agile behaviors

✦ Given keynotes and interactive talks at various conferences worldwide

Throughout his career, Gil has focused on human characteristics that prevent positive outcomes in software development teams. These include limiting habits, fear of change, outdated beliefs, and blind spots. In helping teams overcome these factors, he supports them in reaching ever-higher levels of performance, confidence, and accomplishment. In 2012, he published *The Human Side of Agile*, the definitive guide to leading Agile teams. Later, he designed two innovative self-study courses, *Individuals and Interactions* and *Packing List for Your Agile Journey*.

Gil provides workshops, consulting, facilitation services, and enablement programs to fix lackluster Agile attempts and support ongoing Agile improvement efforts. In addition, he offers much-needed services to help ScrumMasters, team leaders, and managers grow as servant leaders. He is in high demand by organizations looking to fully realize Agile's potential.

Want a taste of what makes Gil different? Receive Gil's popular (and free!) *Something Happened on the Way to Agile* mini-program by visiting **OnTheWaytoAgile.com**. Consisting of 20 daily training segments, it will help you break the cycle of Agile mediocrity and move toward the promised benefits of Agile.